MODERN COOKING

MODERN
COOKING

FROM THE FIRST BACK-STREET
BISTROS OF LYONS TO THE FINEST
RESTAURANTS OF TODAY

—

DREW SMITH

SIDGWICK & JACKSON
LONDON

For Beatrice and Susan
Thanks

First published in 1990 by
Sidgwick & Jackson Limited
1 Tavistock Chambers, Bloomsbury Way
London WC1A 2SG

ISBN 283 99997 7

Typeset in Great Britain by
Rowland Phototypesetting Limited
Bury St Edmunds, Suffolk
Printed in Great Britain by
Billing and Sons Ltd, Worcester

'In 1732, an Englishman called Richard Lucas
opened the first English tavern in Paris. He offered cold
meats and plum pudding (self-service). In 1862, Augis
moved the establishment to Place de la Madeleine, and
called it Restaurant Lucas. In 1925, the new proprietor,
Francis Carton, president of the *Societé des Cuisiniers de
France*, added his name to that of the establishment.'
New Larousse Gastronomique.

In 1985, Lucas Carton was taken over by Alain Senderens.

CONTENTS

BEGINNINGS . . .

*The history of a nation's table is a reflection of
the civilization of that nation*

ESCOFFIER

—

THE BIG MAN looks uncomfortable sitting, as if most of the important things in his life have happened when he has been on his feet. The chair is too tight; the barrel torso swells through the arms, strong from generations of lifting. The features, now cruelly symbolic, have taken on the curves of the cockerel: the nose hooks into a beak, the chest puffs, the large stomach sweeps neatly between the legs. The walk is a strut.

The fat hands, claws, are clasped in front of him on the table. He is staring straight ahead. The back is militarily straight. He is speaking French because, for all his recognition, he speaks only the two languages to which he was born, the other being the cooking. There is none of the reputed image of the playboy. No smoking-jacket sauvity. Rather a masculine camaraderie, in the mould of a union official, or an Eastern bloc party potentate; which in a sense is what he has become.

The name is Bocuse. For seven generations, his family have been *cuisiniers*. His inheritance was to be the public face of a craft that, before him, was set apart.

Although necessarily placed in basements and backrooms, as a craft cooking has been resilient, enterprising, and, surprisingly perhaps, consistent. It has, in its way, spoken for its time and area. It has had to do with what we have been able to scratch off the earth's surface, and with our relationship with all that is around us. Often, its canvas has been so huge that the edges have been hard to discern.

The restaurant has been dismissed as an elitist catwalk of the rich. And sometimes, accepted, that is what it has become. But in a rural agricultural society, as still exists in much of Europe, the restaurant is sponsor and advertiser of the local food economy, and a fundamental part of the economic equation. In England, inns and taverns fulfilled this role until the war, offering a cuisine both identifiable and fluent, before it was dismantled in one of the great abandonments of the twentieth century.

British cooking was a cooking of the seasons: the first lambs and asparagus in May; the salmon and strawberries of high summer; the first grouse of August, and then later, the full range of game (including duck). The fixed points of the cooking were set by the calendar: sage and onion stuffing for summer; apple sauce for autumn; the hard cheeses of late summer, after the cattle had been let out on to the lush summer grazing. Through the leaner, winter times, diet was sustained with baking; but for the other half of the year it must have been a rich cuisine. It is this we have lost.

Yet 100 years earlier, the British contribution to the food of Europe and the world was equal to that of the French and the Italians. The British input, however, was less in the kitchen, but a stage back down the food chain. They bred the pigs, the cattle and the sheep that were to populate the new worlds. Who would say that men like the Harris Brothers, who created the modern idea of bacon; or Hugh Watson, who first bred the Aberdeen Angus were not, in their way, equally important as cooks like Carême, Escoffier, Point, Fayolle; and the modern generation of such as Senderens, Guérard or Blanc?

This is the story of modern cooking from even earlier, traced along a line that goes back at least 200 years to the first restaurant, and before. On its journey, the craft has picked up a baggage of techniques and thinking, the core of which produce what we might now term good food.

This is a book about professional cooking – which is to say, for the most part, men's cooking. The recipes have been honed back to fundamentals, or else I have left them much as they were given to me. This is not a manual of how to cook, although most of the recipes are not that difficult, since cooking is simply a lot of very small jobs, done one after the other. This is a book about cooking, eating, produce and people. And, because food is so fundamental, it has also come to be about politics, about relationships, about towns and countryside, and about the quality of the way we live.

OVERTURE

——

OYSTERS

THE TWIN TOWERS of the church of Mary the Virgin stand in silent prayer over the exhausted oyster beds at Reculver. The body of the church was dynamited and rebuilt inland to escape a surge tide that has never, in 200 years, quite come. The towers were left as landmarks to the Thames pilots. The Christian ruins date back to 600AD, but somewhere down in the gravel are what is left of the fort the Romans built to protect their harbour, not at the mouth of the estuary as today's map suggests, but to the south.

The great estuary of the River Wantsum was the Roman terminus for trade with the rest of Europe. Two thousand years ago the river cut a swathe through the countryside, separating Thanet from the mainland. The galleys steered a course past the rural villages of Chistlet, Stourmouth, Barton, Menstre and out through Richborough (now Sandwich). Fairly large ships navigated the river up to the sixteenth century, but the shifting silts and the force of the North Sea spring tides gradually filled the gullies and harbour basin, until eventually the flow was strangled and estuary turned to river, river to stream and stream to land.

These same shallow tides had also combed the warm marshlands on the lip of the estuary, picking up seeds and grains in their wash, and delivering them as rich meals for the oysters wallowing in the rivulets.

The Reculver beds were protected in the same way as other great oyster beds, at Marennes or Arcachon, from the open sea. William Lombard in his *Perambulations of Kent* in the sixteenth century declared: 'The Reculver are reputed as farre to pass those at Whitstable as those of Whitstable surmount the rest of the shire in savourie saltiness.'

The Romans packed these oysters into large nets and strapped them to the side of the galleys. They were ferried across the Channel and then on, by ice-laden carts, to the northerly garrisons, or else all the way round Finistère and Biscay to Rome itself. The shells of Kent and Essex oysters have been found in the ruins of Roman villas.

At the time, oysters clung in their millions to the European landmass, a grey staircase down to the seabed. Some grew to the circumference of a dinner plate and lived for more than twenty years.

Oysters taste of the waters in which they fatten. The further north and the purer the waters, the more prized they were. Too far out to sea, and the saline softens the flesh. Too far in, and there is not enough salt for them to survive. Often they grow stronger in fresh waters, away from where they were spawned.

The bickering marriage between Kent and Essex fishermen was held together by the recognition that where Essex favoured spawning, Kent waters offered richer grazing. Thames hoys, low-slung fat-bellied boats, into which the oysters were shovelled, took them straight to London. By the eighteenth century, these boats were so numerous that they formed their own floating street alongside Billingsgate.

From June to August, the tiny oyster spat drift through the creeks until they find something solid on the bed to hold on to. The Greeks encouraged them by throwing broken pieces of porcelain into the river. The Romans used tiles. In Italy and the Caribbean, oysters attach themselves to ropes dangled into the water, or to submarine tree roots. The Pacific oyster almost certainly arrived in Europe on the hull of a Portuguese man-of-war.

There are more than 300 species of oyster, each one christened after its bed. The shell of the city-suit grey European oyster, *ostrea edulis*, is shaped like a fan. The colour of the flesh depends on its environment: the Belon, from Brittany, can be slightly pink; the Marennes produces a greenish-hued oyster from the algae in the water; further south at Arcachon they can be sheet white. The Whitstable is pearly, though lately some have acquired a pistachio hue, perhaps from the nitrates feeding the algae in the water.

Oysters might have been the only taste of the sea available for someone living inland. Packed in barrels, deep shell side down, they seal themselves hermetically and survive a week on their last gulp of water, longer on ice.

They were eaten in unbelievable numbers, hundreds at a sitting. They garnished lavish centrepieces. A Whitstable dish of a head and shoulder of cod arrived completely encircled by the matching grey shells. A menu for the East India Company in 1622 for an oyster dinner reads: roast mutton with oysters, boiled oysters, broiled oysters, oyster pie and pickled oysters.

Oysters were plentiful, cheap and nutritious. Low in calories, high in calcium and in vitamins A and D, to some extent they fulfilled the role that milk has come to play in the modern diet. From early times they enjoyed a romantic reputation of potent imagery: an oyster can poison you (more likely, some people have an allergy or else ate dead oysters); oysters are aphrodisiac (Casanova supposedly ate 150 at a sitting); oysters contain pearls (but not the European oyster). The *Detroit Free Press* published this affectionate tribute in 1889. The allusions and Cockney rhymes suggest it was probably English, and it shows how many more different ways of cooking were in use at the time.

L et us royster with the oyster – in the shorter days and moister,
  That are brought by brown September, with its roguish final R;
For breakfast or for supper, on the under shell or upper,
Of dishes, he's the daisy, and of shellfish he's the star.

We try him as they fry him, and even as they pie him;
We're partial to him luscious in a roast:
We boil him and broil him, we vinegar-and-oil him,
And O he is delicious stewed on toast.

We eat him with tomatoes, and the salad with potatoes,
Nor look him o'er with horror when he follows the coldslaw.
And neither does he fret us, if he marches after lettuce
And abreast of cayenne pepper when his majesty is raw.

So welcome with September to the knife and glowing ember,
Juicy darling of our dainties, dispossessor of the clam!
To the oyster, then a hoister, with him a royal royster
We shall whoop it through the land of heathen jam.

THICK, SHUDDERING MEDIUMS

Despite the beautiful names of the American oysters – the Bluepoints, the Crystal Rivers, the Fire Island Salts – cooks favoured the robuster, more brutal techniques – stews, fritters, loaves, roasts, fries, broils and fricassees – as if either they lacked confidence in the oysters' freshness and quality, or they had so many, they could experiment at will.

English cooking of the middle ages suggests similar abundance, even glut. Whole barrels must have been disinterred at a sitting. The seasonings were vibrant, and often the oyster itself became a seasoner, just like garlic in Provence, and as it still is in Chinese cooking.

Oysters appear filling pies with butter, anchovy, breadcrumbs, parsley, pepper, nutmeg, lemon, egg yolk and the liquor; in scooped out bread rolls mixed with the crumbs and cream and crisped in an oven; stewed in butter with parsley and chives, put back in their wiped shells, topped with breadcrumbs and browned off under the grill; simmered in strong broths, even in ales (not so unlikely, as stout was as traditional in beer areas as champagne in wine regions); seasoned with ginger, pepper, cinnamon and thickened with breadcrumbs; or in red wine with fish stock, herbs, anchovies, a few minced oysters to cook down and the flesh and coral of a lobster. Even these fish stocks were often gelatinous, thick, shuddering mediums, using eel and skate. Cheeses are also found: Parmesan to gratinate; mornay; even Stilton and laver in south Welsh borders. Before that, surely, it would have been ewes' milk cheese.

In the strong lambing areas of the coastal downs, they combined with meat, cooked in a mutton broth, or in a Gower recipe which sets the oysters in a jelly of the poor man's cut of sheep's feet, seasoned with mace and thickened with rice. Sausages were fashioned with minced loin of mutton, chopped oysters, breadcrumbs, egg yolks, suet, onion and lemon.

Oyster-pickling was a cottage industry on the Glamorgan coast at the end of the last century. The jars were sold to London at two shillings for 100, twice the price of fresh. John Murel, writing in 1617, promises that oysters will keep up to a year if simmered swiftly in a liquid of red wine, vinegar and their own liquor, the oysters taken out and the liquid allowed to cool before they are put back.

A clear theme of early recipes was that oysters needed one definite, delineating seasoning. In some areas this was often sweet, and not the peppers favoured in England. A vogue in New York was to sift a little sugar on a raw oyster, a habit attributed to a Chinese chef. The Romans used honey. Apicius gives a recipe for a seasoning of pepper, lovage, egg yolk, vinegar, the liquor, oil, wine and honey. An early, out of character, English recipe for a pie follows the idea of combining oysters with layers of boiled parsnips, hard-boiled eggs and lemon; baked for half an hour and served with melted butter and lemon.

DECLINE AND POLLUTION

The oyster beds encircled the English coast like a giant horseshoe until the end of the last century. Humberside, Fleetwood, Anglesey, the Bristol Channel, Hampshire, Sussex, Medway all traded, as well as the better known creeks that survive now in Essex, Kent and Cornwall.

The railways acted like a giant pulley-and-well, dragging them from the sea bed and carrying them directly to the hungry cities. Cottage industries that had plodded along in much the same way for centuries were transformed. The beds were stripped.

While the trade in oysters accelerated, oyster-eating reached its height. 'The European oyster's natural destiny,' Escoffier declared, 'is to be eaten raw.' Escoffier elaborated with a second definition, this time of the word *de luxe*: a pastry vol-au-vent filled with caviar, topped with an oyster, and served with a squeeze of lemon.

Strangely, though, at this time it was the London street stalls that were said to be the best places to buy. 'As the capital of the owner of the stall is small, so too is his stock,' John R. Philpots wrote in 1890. These stalls were the contemporaries and forerunners of the city's great oyster bars and restaurants, which opened as the railways arrived with ever more regular supplies. Some survive even now – Sweetings opened in 1840, Sheekeys in 1896, Bentleys in 1916, Wheelers in 1956, Rules in 1798, Dirty Dicks in 1648.

The Edwardian conception of oysters served shucked on a grand silver salver on ice and the seaweed in which they were packed; with wedges of lemon, salt, pepper, tabasco and a small, two-pronged fork for easing the sweet adductor muscle off the shell, is a vivid image of a period in British cooking: grandiose, cold, virgin produce, offered at its peak accompanied by violently peppery condiments.

But the oyster beds were being decimated, not because they had been over-farmed, since with good management and careful harvesting, the beds revive and even thrive on cultivation. What almost certainly destroyed the breeding stocks, was the pollution that came with industrialization. The beds were poisoned. By the early 1980s, even the Royal Whitstable had run out of natives, and has been re-laid with the more angular, crenellated, phallus-shaped Pacifics and Portuguese. These are a different strain, *crassostrea angulata*.

This sturdier breed has been used recently to re-stock beds, because it is resistant to some of the diseases that have wiped out native oysters at different times round the Continental land mass.

Its tale, as told by the American food writer Waverley Root, is that the trader *Morlaien*, bound from Lisbon probably to Bristol or London, was becalmed in the Bay of Biscay in 1868. In the heat, its cargo of oysters began to go off. The captain could not stand the stench, and ordered the oysters to be jettisoned. But far from all being dead, there were more than enough to revive in the mild, warm waters and create a new industry for the delighted and amazed local fishermen.

The result of the oyster's decline, was that it bowed out of all but the grandest of restaurant menus, and became the luxury which it is perceived to be today. The cooked oyster went out of vogue almost completely, with two isolated exceptions: one Irish, the oysters poached briefly and served with a reduction of Guinness mixed with cream; the other, cooked in hotels, using the same sauce, but made with champagne. But in a converted wine bar overlooking Wandsworth Common a young York-shireman, Marco Pierre White, created a dish in 1986 that was part of a much wider shift; a re-awakening of ideas. The cooking had woken up, after a long period of self-induced hibernation. The mood and vision had changed. Here is a dish that is sophisticated, warm, complex but bal-anced. The four key components play off each other. Colours contrast: white of the inside of the shell, cream of pasta, beige of oyster, green of cucumber, black of caviar; so do the shapes: thin lengths of pasta and cucumber, ovoids of oyster; acidity from the cucumber and the sauce.

A TAGLIATELLI OF OYSTERS AFTER
MARCO PIERRE WHITE

THE SAUCE: Dice 1 shallot per person and sweat in 1 tablespoon white wine vinegar. Add a little water. Reduce, so there is barely any liquid around the softened shallot. Take off the heat and whisk in 2oz butter, a piece at a time. Set aside to infuse for 20 minutes. Season and strain.

THE PASTA: Mix 1lb 4oz plain flour with salt and olive oil. Add 4 size 1 eggs and 6 yolks to bind. Knead. Cut into 8 pieces. Wrap each in cling film and rest in the fridge 30 minutes. Roll out the pasta. Hang across a broom handle to dry for 5–10 minutes. Cut into fine strips. Divide into individual servings, and plunge into boiling water with oil and salt. Allow 1 minute for the water to come back to the boil, and another 2 to cook, depending on thickness. Drain. Rinse. Drain. Mix with a little olive oil.

THE GARNISH: Peel and seed cucumber. Cut into julienne. Poach in a pan with 1 teaspoon butter and a little water.

THE OYSTERS: Wash the shells in hot water. Poach the oysters in their own juice for 15 seconds, allowing 6 per person.

TO SERVE: Put a little water and butter in a pan, throw in enough pasta for one oyster. Stir round with a fork. Lay the pasta in the bottom of the oyster shell. Season. Lay the oyster on top; then the cucumber. Pour over the sauce. Garnish with caviar.

Visually, the pyramid rises from the inedible rocky shell through degrees of translucence up to the tiny, most precious pinnacle, in total a precise chain reaction, long removed from the tradition of messy, substance-giving soups. The difference is 200 years. In that time, a craft and an idea had been forged that were to dominate thinking on food and restaurants, first in Europe and, eventually, in much of the world. The development of those ideas is traced through this book. But first, we must meet some of the key players.

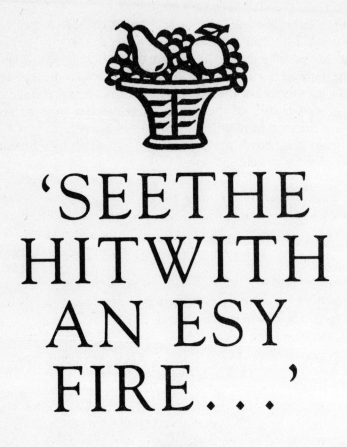

'SEETHE HITWITH AN ESY FIRE...'

—

A SHORT HISTORY OF THE RESTAURANT

THE STORY OF food is also the story of transport. The Romans created a sophisticated food economy through the slaves who built straight roads and rowed their galleys. The anarchy that followed closed down their trade routes and shut the door on the spice markets of Asia. The dark and middle ages moved at the pace of the pack horse trains and the sheep drover, or, slower still, of the gaggles of geese that were walked from Norfolk to market in London.

On main trade roads there were inns, run often by a husband and wife, and offering a communal meal for up to fifty and space to sleep. Away from such routes, it was deemed part of a villager's Christian duty to feed passing strangers. Monasteries were a preferred place to stay. Even before Norman times many, especially in the north, had well-husbanded estates. A rich or notable visitor could expect to be lavishly entertained, though other visits barely show on the church documents, and might have amounted to little but space to sleep and the utensils with which to cook on the monastery fire.

In towns, food was sold on the streets. People ate on the move, or else took food back to where they lodged. The taverns in England, and the early cabarets of middle Europe, where food and drink were part of the entertainment, were the first incarnations of the restaurant.

The taverns sold mostly meats: usually mutton, sometimes beef, boiled or roasted. The diet along the drove roads was monotonous, and varied from one area to the next only by the sauces and relishes put out to go with the meats, hence Worcester Sauce and Yorkshire relish. These are both now credited to as late as 1837, and bear the stamp of the Indian trade, containing tamarind to give them their blackness along with molasses, but for years before that they were locally made and would have been quite distinct and different, as they were one means the inn keeper – or, usually, his wife – had to attract custom.

Slices were hacked off whole carcasses, laid across thick wedges of bread, stiffened in front of the roasting fire. Over them were ladled soup, that might have been anything from a thin gruel, even water in hard times; to a broth in which the mutton had cooked, or to milk and even cream in dairy areas.

TEAS, BROTHS AND GRATINS

This was basic cookery, an essential plank to much of the diet. In poor areas, the gruel might have been filled out with cereals or flour. But at other times, the broth was thick with whatever had been in the larder.

Early recorded variations show a housekeeperly desire to make use of everything that happened to be in the larder on a market day. A 1691 French recipe for a restaurant – being a broth that restored – uses beef, mutton, veal, capon, squabs, partridges, onions, root vegetables and herbs, sealed hermetically with a paste and flour mix inside a pot without any liquid. The pot was then lowered into a larger, water-filled vat, and simmered for five to six hours over an open fire.

Two hundred years earlier, Andrew Boorde recorded this, more direct, distillation in England.

BEEF TEA CIRCA 1500

Take a grete glasse (pot) and do thi beef therein, and do onyone mynced and whole cloves and maces and pouder of pepur, and lay splinters in the bottom (of the pot), that the flesh hit not, and stop it well, that no eyrie go outie, and seethe hitwith an esy fire – (or) seethe it in a pot with water in a cawdron, but top it well that no eyre goo oute.

Such teas and stocks were the province of the professional kitchen, while the bread has stayed part of home cooking. Recipes for gratins can barely have changed, though this one from Somerset in the 1950s smacks of aggrandizement for the purposes of publication.

SOMERSET FARMHOUSE GRATIN

Slice 1 onion. Sweat in butter. Add flour, then 1 pint milk. Season with mustard. Add 4oz grated Cheddar and 4 sliced hard-boiled eggs. Serve on toast.

Bargees on the Shropshire Union Canal cooked a dish they called brewis: frying a slice of bread in butter, seasoning it with salt and pepper, covering with cheese, usually Cheshire which would have been the cargo, and spooning over water or stock. A Yorkshire strategy was to take the tea left over from the night before and use it to deglaze the breakfast pan of bacon, eggs and bread cooked in the bottom of the range.

THE ARRIVAL OF THE POTATO

The potato, rather than bread, has survived as the base of the gratin for modern restaurant usage. Some people have wrongly ascribed the name Dauphinois to the not implausible idea that it was a dish created by a chef for the dauphin. Far more likely, the name derives from the Dauphine in the lower Alps, near the Hermitage vineyards, well-known for the quality of its milk and cheeses such as Saint-Marcellin and also for other gratin dishes, using noodles, other root vegetables and even crayfish.

GRATIN DAUPHINOIS

Peel 1½lb waxy, yellow potatoes. Slice thinly, soak and dry. Rub an earthenware dish lushly with butter. Season with garlic, nutmeg. Lay the potatoes in the dish so it is up to three-quarters full, seasoning each layer at a time. Pour over ½ pint of cream. Put in a roasting oven for 1–1½ hours, lifting to the top of the oven at end to form a good brown crust.

Subtle shifts in ingredients, types of butter and cream, variety of potato and thickness of slices, extent of the seasoning, heat of the oven, produce markedly different results which have, over time, acquired their own, often disputed, identities. From the same family are plainly Savoyard – in one variation, a dauphinois using only veal stock in place of cream, in others using a consommé – and Gruyère, although other cheeses from the Savoie like Reblochon, Vacherin or a mature Tomme might be logical. For it is this Alpine strip of eastern France that must also have been one of the first hosts to the newly imported tubers after they arrived from South America in the mid-sixteenth century.

Most identifiable as a specific restaurant variation is Pommes Anna, where cream is not used at all, only butter. It was reputedly created at the fashionable Café Anglais in Paris, which opened in 1802.

WATERSHEDS

BY THE END of the seventeenth century, the different threads of agriculture, trade, cooking began to wrap around each other into a recognizable twine. The towns and cities began to assert their politics. Recipes started to take on familiar conceits. The modern era was about to take hold.

Ports had become places of some size and attraction. Not only did the ships bring in new produce, but the markets drew the foods from across the country to be loaded for export. And it was in the ports, certainly in England, that what is now called English cooking was formed. To a lesser extent the same argument could be put forward for France, with Marseilles in the south, Nantes in the west, and Caen and Le Havre in the north.

For England, the culinary line was clear. Cumberland rum butter took its cinnamon, nutmeg, rum and brown sugar straight off the boats that plied their trade to the West Indies and Whitehaven. Plum pudding is schizophrenic: one half imported – raisins, currants, candied mixed peel, brandy, cloves, cinnamon, nutmeg, coriander, lemon peel, sugar – and the other native – beef suet, chopped apples, flour, breadcrumbs, eggs, milk – combined in the deeply British technique of wrapping in a cloth and boiling as a bag for four-and-a-half hours.

Oranges had their own warehouse at Hunstrete in the east end of London, and slipped easily into the cooking as jellies, syrups, fritters, sauces, marmalades. The Essex jam towns of Elsenham and Tiptree were close enough to profit. Boodles Orange Fool, created at the Boodles club in St James which, along with the other gentlemen's clubs in the nineteenth century, was the cutting edge of English cooking, is as well known as it is simple: mix the juice of four oranges and two lemons with a pint of double cream and three tablespoons of sugar; spread over a sponge; garnish with the rind and chill for two hours.

Urban cooking had its own energy. First the canals and then, far more importantly, the railways opened up the inland markets and the last of the impenetrable areas. The feudal world's horizons had been of rural, unchanging parishes, villages and small parcels of land, but now it was possible to look much further. The sea-going economy had turned full circle, and was about to spin the other way. Ships started to take homesteaders, cereals and stud animals back, to colonize the new worlds.

The politics of the last 200 years began to form, in the shape of the relationship between the country and the town, the farmer and the industrialist, the feeder and the fed. For the first time it was possible for a majority of people not to spend their entire working day producing food to eat. Land ceased to be the only way of life for most people, and instead of being an outward symbol of wealth and status became the means by which wealth and status could be generated. The urban market was now big enough to make this possible. The new world was also becoming important. No longer was it just somewhere to plunder, now it was a trade centre to colonize and exploit.

England and France reacted differently to the changed world. In England, the enclosure laws passed from 1760 drove millions off the land. Dispossessed, the peasantry drifted into the new cities to find work; were conscripted into the army to fight Napoleon; or emigrated to the new world. For 100 years the landowning farmers had the world their own way.

This was their golden age until, ironically, in the 1880s the descendants of the same people who had been evicted from their tenancies began to export grain from America and Canada back to Europe, and the economy turned again. But for much of that time English peasants might well have wondered if they would not have done better to have followed the example of their French counterparts, whose revolution had at least left many with their farms and homes and the means of survival.

THE TERROR

Revolution was the catalyst for the French kitchen. Food was at the heart of the terror. The French aristocracy had been greedy and mendacious, demanding not just a share of the foods the villages produced, but also laying claim to wild game in the forests. Their hubris was to want to own the world, and everything in it.

There was a fundamental and unstated affinity between the peasant and the kitchen. To be able to eat, and to eat well, seemed to become a reassurance that the revolution had been worthwhile. And because France is so much bigger than Britain, the importance of agriculture in the political consensus was proportionately larger.

The delegates to the new republic brought to Paris their own customs, foods, and ways of cooking. The capital became harbour to a fleet of different cookings from all the various departments. Paris wore them like the medals of campaigns. The combustion that created these early restaurants was political revolution. There was a need, not just for places to eat, but also for places to meet.

To the professional chef, though, revolution had meant one thing: unemployment. Even in the eighteenth century, many had come to work in Britain, where the political climate was calmer and where things French were the vogue. Come the revolution, chefs who had stayed behind found their employers homeless and headless. So, they took their cooking to the street. A whole cuisine, fashioned for the ceremonies and grand spectacles of the now gutted and ransacked chateaux, had to be scaled down and re-defined.

The kitchen, perhaps above all else, was charged with making sense of the trauma of revolution and life in the new republic.

THE FIRST RESTAURANT

The first restaurant to take the name was in the Rue Poulies in Paris and pre-dated the revolution. The feudal food crafts were dominated by guilds, some of which dated back to the thirteenth century. The most powerful of all were the *traiteurs*, who held up the introduction of the restaurant for centuries. They alone had the licence to sell different meats in different sauces. Roasters could only roast, and were prevented from making stews or casseroles. The *charcutiers* – from *chair-cuitiers*, the flesh-cookers – could only cure meats and make pâtés, but were not allowed to kill the pigs themselves, which was the province of yet another guild. Auberges, which were in any case reviled for their poor food, served set, unrefined communal meals; while cafés were constrained to selling ices and *pâtisseries*.

The *traiteurs'* hold was so rigidly policed, that they could even sell on the liquids in which they cooked their meats to soup sellers. Their only competitors were the hawkers, who sold the leftovers of the big house banquets.

It was Boulanger, a soup merchant, who added to his menu in 1762 or 1765 a dish of sheep's feet in white wine sauce, and advertised his business in Latin: *Venite ad me, omnes qui stomacho laboritis et ego restaurabo vos*. The restaurant was christened.

The *traiteurs* sued. In what the *Larousse Gastronomique* calls a 'solemn judgement of Parliament', they were overruled. Monsieur Boulanger's little restaurant, with its uncovered, marble-topped tables, was celebrated. The sheep's feet were sent to Versailles for Louis XV to taste. Louis, who was doubtless used to rather more rarefied cooking than that of the Rue Poulies, was under-impressed. Not so everyone else. The menu expanded to include poached poultry with coarse salt; fresh eggs and broth. The style was set. Boulanger, who could not have been such a simple fellow after all, being familiar with Latin and having the nous to take on the culinary establishment, had one other ace up his sleeve: the customers had their own tables, and did not have to share as they did in the auberges. By the end of the century, there were 500 such places in Paris alone.

By 1776, all the guild licences had been thrown out. The first grand restaurant was La Grande Taverne de Londres at 26 Rue de Richelieu, opened by Antoine Beauvilliers. The name was a tribute to all things fashionably English.

THE FIRST RESTAURANTS, ACCORDING TO LAROUSSE

1582 La Tour d'Argent

1732 Lucas

1759   La Mère Guy
1763–5 Boulanger
1765   Michel Bocuse
1773   Cadran Bleu
1783   Beauvilliers
1784   Mère Saguet
1786   Les Frères Provencaux
1797   Cafè Hardy
         Maison Dorée 1841

| Carême |
| 1784–1833 |

1800–1860   Rocher de Cancale
1802   Foyòt
1802–1913   Café Anglais

1820   Maison Dauphin
     Magny 1842
     Taverne Anglais 1845
     Noel Peters 1854

| Escoffier |
| 1847–1935 |

1865 Restaurant Lucas   1877   Maison Marguery
                       Savoy 1896
                       Carlton 1898

1925 Lucas Carton

1985 Alain Senderens

1990 La Tour d'Argent

CARÊME: THE GRANDFATHER OF THE CUISINE

MARIE-ANTOINE (ANTONIN) CARÊME (1784–1833), came to be seen as the figurehead of this renaissance, the grandfather of modern cooking, and the chef who handed on the cuisine of the grand, pre-revolution aristocracy to the restaurant and hotel chefs of the nineteenth century. His biography reads like a memo to Cecil B. de Mille. He was not just a poor urchin, he was one of fifteen. They were so poor, that his father took him out to dinner in a tavern when he was ten and told him not to come home again. They were so miserable, his father told him, that he would have a better chance out on his own.

And so he did. Not just for his cooking, especially his confections, nor for his diplomacy, but because in his last years he wrote his cooking down and left a tangible bridge between two eras of history. The French writer Jean-Francois Revel said of him: 'Carême introduced to the cooking what, in painting, is called allied values. He understood for the first time that the flavours and smells had to be judged, not in the absolute, but in their relationship with each other.' Carême himself noted that over his life, sauces had become more distinct through the use of infusions and reductions of stocks, and the use of cooked, rather than raw flours in a roux.

After his father put him on the street, the young Carême found work in a nearby cook shop. He was a skilful apprentice and graduated quickly to the well-known *pâtissier* Bailly, in Rue Vivienne. Here, he was allowed to create what must have been spectacular visual effects.

At night, he studied in libraries, copying the etchings and sketches of old buildings which he then recreated in sugar, nougat, marzipan and meringue. Pastry and confection were the great arts for him, superior almost to what we now call cuisine. 'The fine arts,' he wrote, 'are five in number: painting, sculpture, poetry, music and architecture – whose main branch is confectionery.' After a spell freelancing and running his own *pâtisserie*, in 1804 he went to work for one of his richest and most powerful admirers, Prince Talleyrand, Napoleon's foreign minister. Talleyrand took him out of the restaurant arena and into the world of embassies and kings. Together, they developed a vision of cooking as a tool of diplomacy. They created banquets to impress and persuade. Their table was a statement of French wealth, ambition and culture. Dinner was propaganda.

Perhaps the revolution still needed a hero in the same mould as in the *ancien régime*, for Carême went on to work for George IV when he was Prince Regent; Czar Alexander in St Petersburg; the British embassy in Paris; and finally, Baron de Rothschild.

THE FIRST MENUS

While Carême cooked for kings, the new art of restauration flourished in Paris. Across the city, chefs began to give their names not just to restaurants, but also to dishes, where 100 years before they would have named them after their patrons. At the Café Anglais, Dugléré gave his name to sole shallow-poached on a bed of chopped onion, shallot, tomato and parsley, with a small glass of good white wine. The fish was taken out and filleted while the sauce was made by reducing the cooking liquor by half, building it up again with fish velouté, and finishing with butter and a squeeze of lemon.

In 1877, Marguery took over the Maison Dauphin. He wanted a dish that would be as well known as Dugléré's. This was what he achieved:

FILLETS OF SOLE MARGUERY

THE FUMET: Fillet 2 fine soles. Use the bones and trimmings to make a white wine fumet, flavoured with a little chopped onion, a sprig of thyme, quarter of a bay leaf and a little parsley. Season with salt and pepper. Simmer for 15 minutes. Add to this fumet, which should be strained and concentrated, the strained cooking liquor of 1 litre of mussels cooked in white wine.

THE FISH: Place the fillets of sole, floured and lightly flattened, on a buttered baking dish. Sprinkle over a few tablespoons of the fumet. Cover with buttered greaseproof paper and poach gently. Drain the fillets well. Set them in an oval dish and surround with a double row of shelled mussels and shrimps. Keep hot while the sauce is prepared.

THE SAUCE: Add the cooking juices of the sole to the fumet and strain. Boil down by two-thirds. Remove from the heat, allow the sauce to cool a little, then add 6 egg yolks. Whisk the sauce over a gentle heat, like a hollandaise, incorporating 350g of the finest butter, slightly melted. Season the sauce and strain. Coat the fillets and brown in a hot oven.

Other restaurants were known for individual dishes. The Café de Paris, which opened in 1822, created lobster thermidor; Noel Peters' lobster

Américaine was named after one of the American partners; The Maison Dorée for its bouillabaisse; Magny for its chateaubriand; Mère Saguet, which opened as early as 1784, for stewed cow's udders; Vefour for its chicken fricassee *à la Marengo*. The Taverne Anglaise, which opened in 1845 on the Route de la Revolte, offered roast beef and Yorkshire pudding. There were queues on holidays and feast days.

This elite, working in a relatively small area of the city and supported by a host of smaller, unrecorded bistros, eateries and even street stalls offering regional and bourgeois cooking, founded a dynasty.

THE TWIN LIGHT

ACROSS THE WATER, a still smaller clique found sanctuary in London's clubs and hotels. It included the flamboyant Alexis Soyer, who cooked first at the Reform Club and then for the troops in Crimea and for London's poor, with a soup kitchen in Farringdon Road; and later Escoffier himself. London became Paris's twin light, a side show for the new theatre. But here, the process of change was slower.

In the 1830s and '40s, London had a thriving street economy in food such as it had had in medieval times. Ham sandwiches were sold outside theatres; potatoes were baked, having previously been roasted like chestnuts, and had suddenly become a more profitable line than fruits; sheep's trotters were a common source of meat, now sold to the street markets instead of the glue makers; fried fish and bread were hawked on brightly coloured trays. A poor man's diet might have come from the coffee stall for breakfast; shellfish for lunch, hot eels or pea soup; cakes and tarts in the afternoon; and, in the evening, a meat pudding or a trotter.

Little of this had so far penetrated indoors. The class distinction was succinct, in that the rich had access to dining-rooms and the poor did not. One hundred years after Monsieur Boulanger's first restaurant, *Cassells Domestic Dictionary* still stiffly defined a restaurant as a 'modern French name for an eating house . . . in our metropolis restaurants have been introduced, to which foreigners and other persons resort who prefer the French method of cooking'.

The first recipe in *The Cook's Guide* by Queen Victoria's chef Elme Francatelli, dated 1888, contains almost as many ingredients as the tavern stock pot of 200 years before. Although English by birth, Francatelli had worked with Carême, and succeeded Soyer at the Reform. He gives an evocative description of the kind of labour involved in cooking, which would have been physically more on a par with a job like welding. The liquid is cooked right down and then built up again, where most kitchens would simply roast off the meats and work from there.

THE STOCKPOT AFTER ELME FRANCATELLI

Place in a well-tinned stock pot, capable of containing about 8 gallons, about 10lb of leg or shin of beef and an equal weight of knuckles of veal, cut into pieces; to these add the carcass of an old hen and a knuckle of ham; moisten with 2 quarts of broth or water; set the stockpot to boil down sharply, until the liquid has become reduced to a glaze. The heat must then be slackened by placing ashes upon the fire in order to abate its fierceness, so as to allow the glaze to attain a light brown colour, without it being burnt and carbonized; if this latter accident happen, it tends to considerably diminish the stomachic qualities and flavour of the stock and consommé.

As soon as the consolidation of the glaze is effected, make up the fire, fill up the stock pot and when it boils, skim it thoroughly; after which garnish with 6 carrots, 4 onions, 3 turnips, 4 leeks, 2 heads of celery, an onion in which 12 cloves have been stuck; season with 3oz salt, and having allowed the stock to continue gently boiling for about 5 hours, remove the grease from its surface; and then proceed to strain it through a sieve into clean pans for use as directed herein after . . .

ESCOFFIER: THE ERA OF THE GRAND HOTEL

GEORGES AUGUSTE ESCOFFIER (1846–1935) brought the creative effort of the nineteenth century into focus. Like Carême, although a master *cuisinier* himself, his reputation rests on his writing. The *Guide Culinaire*, published in 1903, which he compiled with Philéas Gilbert, Apollon Caillat and Emile Fétu, is indisputably the most important gastronomic work to date: a dictionary in a world of romances and novels. Ninety years on, large tracts still remain an essential, perhaps the single, thesis.

The *Guide* took twenty years to compile. Gilbert, known for his bouts of temper and his attacks on the sculptural pomposities of classical cooking, was chef with Bonvalet, one of the best restaurants in Paris from 1884 to 1920. Caillat had worked in the south and around Lyons, even cooking for Queen Victoria when she summered at Aix-les-Bains. He brought the regional influence, and encouraged Escoffier, who was from Provence and had worked at Monte Carlo and Nice before moving north, not to disregard his own roots. The first edition was published in November 1902. Escoffier re-edited it four times in the next twenty years and, just before his death, oversaw a popularized version prepared by his friend Prosper Montagné, another accomplished Parisian chef, for the publishers Larousse. As with Carême, he made much of trying to simplify.

Bear in mind that the classical kitchen was still steeped in the idea of banquets and festivals, and the talk of creating a less elaborate cooking was as much to do with the presentations as the dishes themselves.

The compromise of the recipe appealed to the classical kitchen in its attempt to bring order to the anarchy that surrounded it. The recipe was well suited to the idiom: ingredients held in bondage, submitted to torturous, disfiguring disciplines that disguised their origins. There was a place for all these transmogrifications to be chronicled, so that disciples who came later would not need to deviate from the path. The *Guide* consecrated the rituals.

Earlier cookery books, before the *Guide*, had for the most part presented a different, very insular perspective. With few exceptions, they represented a cooking peculiar to the genteel, leisured, servanted, affluent, who had both access to print and the time to write it all down. The authors were not cooks. They had other people to cook for them. The many editions of Mrs Beeton, or the capricious recipes of Eliza Acton or any of the other good women who diligently recorded the recipes of upper middle class life, stemmed from a class and experience that set the authors apart from the professional cook. The heat of the tavern kitchen, or the breathless hurly-burly of the cabarets, where there might have been a direct link into the native cooking, were just not there.

The true root of English regional cooking, that is to say the cooking of the rural poor, was probably left behind in the migration from the villages. But in France, it survived along with the peasant farmers and in the revolutionary restaurants, because food had become patriotic. Cooking was institutionalized into the fabric of society, in a role later taken on by money.

But Escoffier was part of the profession. He had started work at twelve, and where Carême had been called the king of chefs and chef to the kings, Escoffier was dubbed the emperor. He lived to be eighty-eight and spent sixty-two years working, which in part accounts for his awesome reputation.

His medium was the grand hotel. Their customers were his. Peach Melba, now reduced to a grim pastiche of peaches and cream in every seaside café, was created for the diva Nellie Melba after the first act of *Lohengrin*. The peaches were served on vanilla ice cream in the figure of a swan carved in ice, frosted in sugar and floating on a silver salver. The Savoy and the Carlton gave him space, investment, huge brigades and rich customers. Here was a scale similar to that of the grand aristocratic houses. The well-off were moving. They needed places to travel by boat, train, car; and places to stay when they arrived. Biarritz, Cannes, Monaco, Nice, arrived on the fashionable map. In England it was Torquay, Bournemouth, Brighton. The tyre company Michelin launched its guide to hotels and restaurants in 1900. The railways invested heavily in resorts to persuade people to travel.

THE GUIDE

For cooks, the large brigades that staffed these hotels became the place to train. The whole of the cookery bent to the iron will of the codification. To cook, was to execute the laws as laid down. The *Guide*'s 5,000 clipped recipes became as functional as a medical text book. If it was not in the book, it was not cuisine.

The rigidity of the codification meant the cooking could travel. It was international. And it did not depend overly on the individual skills of a single man. It was team cooking. Techniques could surmount the variations in local markets. The real boundary was only one of climate. Too far south, and the batteries of stock pots and sauces became dangerous in the heat. To the north, it was a tradeable commodity.

THE IMPERIAL STAIRCASE

A S ESCOFFIER COMPILED the *Guide*, he was criticizing chefs for the indeterminate uniformity of their stocks and bases. 'Your sauces,' he declared, 'do not distinguish.'

The key to the *Guide* system was its series of interlocked sauces. Escoffier singled out four pillars as foundations on which nearly everything else could stand: brown stock, veal stock, béchamel and tomato. He said the espagnol, from the brown stock, and the tomato, combined with the cooking juices of a meat provided a perfectly balanced sauce.

Making stock and making wines, might be two arms of the same discipline. The *vigneronne* has his grapes; the chef, his bones. The cooking accelerates the process, where wine is left to mature for months and years; but otherwise there is the same breaking down of an original ingredient, the same blending with other tastes, the same maturation, and the same effort to harmonize the vagaries of the harvest into an essential character.

The parents of the stock are the *pot-au-feu* and gratins. At the first Michelin three-star restaurant in Britain, in the subterranean billiard hall of Le Gavroche in London, Albert Roux has kept a *pot-au-feu* on the menu from the Sixties. The sauce is actually English, from Escoffier. If the meats are to be the central part of the dish, they should go into hot water; if the bouillon is more important, into cold.

POT-AU-FEU SAUCE ALBERT AFTER
ALBERT ROUX

THE MEATS: Bone a shin of beef. Trim the sinews. Tie as for a roast. Blanch in lightly salted water. Trim 3 oxtails. Chop into 2-inch sections. Blanch. Put both in an earthenware cocotte, and cover with well-seasoned white beef bouillon. Simmer 3–4 hours, until tender. Wrap a marrow bone in muslin and add for the last 20 minutes.

THE VEGETABLES: Per person, cook in the broth 2 carrots, 2 turnips, 2 courgettes, 2 leeks, a wedge of cabbage tied with string, until slightly more cooked than *al dente*.

THE PARSNIPS: Peel and slice parsnips. Steam until tender. Purée. Add cream, salt and white pepper.

SAUCE ALBERT: Simmer 5oz grated horseradish in white bouillon for 20 minutes. Thicken with butter sauce, cream and breadcrumbs. Reduce. Sieve. Add 2 egg yolks. Season with salt and pepper. Finish with a teaspoon of mustard and 1 of vinegar.

TO SERVE: Slice a section of meat. Bone 2 sections of tail. Arrange with the vegetables in a deep dish, and cover with the broth. Serve the parsnip purée on the side, with brioche toast topped with a slice of poached bone marrow and the sauce Albert.

The early *pot-au-feu* were chasms, into which any back-of-the-larder item or trimming from the butchery department might fall. In taverns, they were meant to be all-purpose, and often used different meats and seasonings. Such indiscipline offended Escoffier. He needed an accurate and achievable standard, or his cooking had no character or identity. In 1902, he wrote it down as this:

BROWN STOCK AFTER ESCOFFIER

Bone 4lb shin of beef and 4lb knuckle of veal. Break up the bones and roast in the oven. Reserve the meat from the bones. Fry ½lb onions and ½lb carrots in beef dripping. Put the roasted bones, the fried onions and carrots, a knuckle of ham, a rind of pork, parsley, thyme, bay and garlic in a pot with a gallon of cold water. Bring to a simmer. Skim off the scum as it rises to the surface. Cook all day, topping up with more water as the liquid evaporates, and continuing to take off any scum. Fry the boned meats and add to the stock, deglazing the frying pan with the bouillon. Cook for another 2 hours or longer. Sieve. Strain. Taste.

He stressed the sieving and skimming to the point that it was a continuous process, a ritualistic habit for any cook passing just to flick off the froth with a ladle, and stop the impurities nose-diving back into the depths and clouding the final result.

Such stocks would often be cooked for more than a day, or the bouillon would be cooked up again with a new set of vegetables and bones for a more powerful taste.

This brown stock was the mother to the greatest of all his sauce families, espagnol, and its siblings demi-glace and poivrade. On to each of these were constructed flights of different sauces, each discernibly different, although permutations on a theme. His seasonings were cayenne and lemon.

ESPAGNOL: Stir 14 pints brown stock into 1lb 6oz brown roux, set aside. Fry 9oz diced carrots, 5oz diced onions in pork fat, drain and add to stock. Deglaze the pan with white wine, reduce by half, and add to stock. Simmer 1 hour, skimming constantly. Sieve. Add another 3½ pints stock, simmer for 2 more hours, strain, allow to cool. The next day add 4 more pints stock, 4½lb tomatoes, stirring continuously. Simmer 1 hour and strain.

POIVRADE: Sweat a mirepoix. Add vinegar, and most of marinade from meat. Reduce by two-thirds. Add 2 pints espagnol. Simmer 35 minutes. Add peppercorns. Simmer another 10 minutes. Strain. Add the rest of the marinade. Sieve. Skim and simmer 35 minutes. Finish with 2oz butter.

DEMI-GLACE: Reduce espagnol by half. Flavour with sherry, port, Madeira or a fine wine.

NINE SAUCES FROM ESPAGNOL

1 BORDELAISE: Reduce by half, ½ pint red wine with shallots and herbs. Add 1 pint espagnol. Simmer 15 minutes and strain. Finish with a meat glaze, lemon juice and poached bone marrow.

2 **BONNEFOY**: As for bordelaise, but use white wine.

3 **MOELLE**: As for bordelaise, but finish with chopped, poached bone marrow and parsley. If for a vegetable, add butter.

4 **ROUENNAISE (FOR DUCK)**: As for bordelaise, using a good wine. Add a purée of raw duck livers. Sieve.

5 **BRETONNE**: Sauté onions. Add white wine. Reduce by half. Add equal quantities of espagnol and tomato sauce, and a crushed garlic clove. Simmer to amalgamate. Finish with chopped parsley.

6 **HACHÉE**: Sweat onions and shallots. Add 8 fl oz vinegar, reduce by half, add 1 pint espagnol, ¼ tomato sauce, simmer to infuse. Finish with chopped ham, capers, duxelles and parsley.

7 **PIQUANT**: Reduce 8 fl oz white wine with 8 fl oz vinegar and shallots by half. Add 2 pints espagnol. Simmer 10 minutes and skim. Finish with gherkins, tarragon, chervil and parsley.

8 **ROMAINE**: Caramelize 2oz sugar. Dissolve ¼ pint vinegar. Add 1 pint espagnol and 8 fl oz game stock. Reduce by one-quarter. Strain. Finish with pine seed kernels, sultanas and currants.

9 **VIN ROUGE**: Sweat onion and a mirepoix. Moisten with 1 pint of good wine. Reduce by half. Add a clove of crushed garlic and 1¼ pints espagnol. Simmer and skim 15 minutes. Strain. Finish with anchovy essence and cayenne.

FIVE SAUCES FROM POIVRADE

1 **CHEVREUIL**: Sweat bacon or game trimmings in a mirepoix. Add 2 pints poivrade. Simmer. Skim. Strain. Add ¼ pint red wine. Finish with sugar and cayenne.

2 **DIANE**: Reduce poivrade. Whip in 8 fl oz cream. Finish with truffle and the white of hard-boiled egg.

3 **GRAND VENEUR**: Add ¼ pint hare's blood and an equal amount of marinade to 2 pints poivrade. Infuse on the side of the stove. Strain.

4 **MUSCOVITE**: Finish a poivrade sauce made with venison stock, with Malaga wine. Infuse with juniper berries, toasted pine seed kernels (or almonds) and soaked currants.

5 **VENISON**: To 2 pints game poivrade, add 4 fl oz melted redcurrant jelly and ¼ pint cream.

EIGHTEEN SAUCES FROM DEMI-GLACE

1 MUSHROOM: Reduce 8 fl oz mushroom liquor by half. Add 2 pints demi-glace. Simmer. Strain. Finish with butter and button mushrooms.

2 CHASSEUR: Sauté mushrooms and shallots. Add 8 fl oz white wine. Reduce by half. Add 8 fl oz tomato sauce, and 8 fl oz demi-glace. Simmer. Finish with butter, tarragon and chervil.

3 BROWN CHAUD FROID: Reduce 2 pints demi-glace, 2 pints aspic jelly, 4 fl oz truffle essence, 2 fl oz Madeira or port, by one-third. Finish with white wine and strain.

4 DIABLE: Reduce 8 fl oz white wine and shallots by two-thirds. Add 8 fl oz demi-glace. Season with cayenne.

5 FINES HERBES: Infuse parsley, chervil, tarragon and chives in white wine. Add 8 fl oz demi-glace and reduce by one-third. Sieve. Finish with chopped herbs and lemon.

6 TARRAGON: As for Fines Herbes, but using only tarragon.

7 GODARD: Sauté a mirepoix with ham, add 1 pint white wine. Reduce by half. Add 2 pints demi-glace and ¼ pint mushroom liquor. Simmer 10 minutes. Strain. Reduce by one-third. Strain.

8 HUSSARDE: Sweat onions and shallots. Reduce ¼ pint white wine by half. Add 8 fl oz demi-glace, 2 tablespoons tomato purée, 4oz ham, 6 fl oz white stock, garlic and herbs. Simmer 30 minutes. Sieve. Finish with chopped ham, horseradish and parsley.

9 ITALIENNE: Add a duxelles and ham to 2 pints tomato-flavoured demi-glace. Simmer 6 minutes. Finish with tarragon, chervil and parsley.

10 LYONNAISE: Sweat 9oz onions in butter. Add 6 fl oz white wine and an equal amount of vinegar, and reduce by two-thirds. Add 8 fl oz demi-glace. Simmer, skim and sieve.

11 MADÈRE: Reduce 2 pints demi-glace to thicken. Add 4 fl oz Madeira. Strain.

12 PÉRIGUEUX: Season 2 pints demi-glace with ¼ pint truffle essence and 4oz chopped truffle.

13 PORTO: Reduce 2 pints demi-glace to thicken. Add 4 fl oz port. Strain.

14 RÉGENCE: Sauté mirepoix and truffles. Add 8 fl oz Rhine wine. Reduce by half. Add 2 pints demi-glace, simmer, skim and sieve.

15 ROBERT: Sweat onions. Add 12 fl oz white wine. Reduce by two-thirds. Add 2 pints demi-glace. Simmer 10 minutes. Sieve. Finish with sugar and English mustard.

THE CLASSICAL KITCHEN'S BATTERY OF STOCKS AND SAUCES

WHITE STOCK
(Veal shin, chicken, carrot, onion, leek)

WHITE CHICKEN STOCK
(White stock, chicken)

TOMATO SAUCE
(White stock, flour, tomato)

BROWN STOCK
(Roasted beef shin, veal knuckle, pork, carrot, onion)

BROWN VEAL STOCK
(Roasted veal bones, carrots, onions)

BÉCHAMEL
(Milk, flour)

FISH STOCK
(Sole, whiting, brill bones + trimmings, onions, mushrooms, white wine in ratio 1:10 to water)

RED WINE FISH STOCK
(Bones + trimmings from fish, blanched onion, mushroom, red wine in ratio 2:3.5 to water)

GAME STOCK
(Venison, hare, three kinds of bird)

The foundation liquids as listed by Escoffier. Glazes were made by reducing and skimming. For sauces, a roux of flour and butter was nearly always added. The béchamel is the mother of these roux. The brown veal stock was the major gravy. Thickened with arrowroot and reduced by three-quarters, it becomes the multi-purpose *jus de veau lié*, a clean, transparent, light brown juice. The brown stock was the major sauce stock. The red wine fish stock is a practical variation for using the liquid in which a fish has been poached. Essences used the same principles but less liquid to concentrate flavours.

16 SALMIS: Add the skin and carcasses of game and ½ pint white wine to sweated shallot and mirepoix. Reduce by two-thirds. Add 2 pints demi-glace. Simmer 45 minutes. Sieve. Add 12 fl oz game stock and simmer 45 minutes. Add mushroom liquor, truffle essence and finish with butter.

17 TORTUE: Add sage, basil, sweet marjoram, bay, mushroom, rosemary and thyme to 8 fl oz simmering veal stock, and infuse 25 minutes. Add 4 peppercorns and infuse another 2 minutes. Strain. Add to 2 pints demi-glace and 6 fl oz tomato sauce. Reduce by one-quarter. Strain. Finish with 4 fl oz Madeira, truffle essence and cayenne.

18 ZINGARA: Reduce ¼ pint white wine and ¼ pint mushroom liquor by two-thirds. Add 1 pint demi-glace, 8 fl oz tomato sauce and 4 fl oz white stock. Simmer and skim 5 minutes. Finish with cayenne, a julienne of ham, salted ox tongue, mushroom and truffle.

THE MODERN STOCKS

The thick brown stock which runs through all these sauces has been overtaken by a lighter veal stock, whose presence is more subtle, but whose influence can be as pervasive.

Veal bones, being younger, are rich in collagen, which produces gelatine. The flavour is not yet pronounced. The result is a texturous white canvas, on which other flavours can be painted; a sinuous, transparent hand deglazing the caramelized crusts off the bottom of the roasting tray. Occasionally it might be used alone, but more often it is reduced by half and blended with wines or spirits to provide back-lighting for a beef or veal dish, or to amplify another sauce. Taken down by at least one-third to a glace, it saves feeble sauces.

Modern recipes have streamlined the cooking to not much more than breaking up the bones, and simmering for four hours with only the primary aromatics carrot, celery, thyme, parsley. If it is not strong enough, it is reduced.

VEAL STOCK (MODERN)

Break up the bones and roast. Dice onions, carrot, celery thickly, add parsley and thyme. Lay the roasted bones on the vegetables and cover with plenty of water. Bring slowly to a simmer, skimming all the time, and cook slowly for 4 hours. Sieve. Reduce.

THE HINGE ON THE DOOR

B UT FOR ESCOFFIER, his stocks, and therefore his sauces, were all. His was a cooking apart. The regional roots are faintly recognizable, but the variations are rarefied and the resemblance as close as that of a Hollywood star decked in stilettos, furs, dark glasses and diamonds to her sister with six children on a ranch back home in the mid-west.

Take a dish like sole normande. Caen and Dieppe claim the original of sole normande, the fish poached in *cidre bouchée* and the pan deglazed with cream. The technique is less remarkable than the quality of those three ingredients in that area. But in the *Guide*, its namesake has been elevated to an ostentatious piece of exhibitionism credited to Langlais at the Rocher Cancale in Paris, and dated 1837.

SOLE NORMANDE AFTER LANGLAIS

THE SAUCE: To 1 litre fish velouté, add ¼ litre mushroom cooking liquor, the juice in which mussels have cooked, and 1½ litres stock made with the bones of the sole and thickened with egg yolks and cream. Reduce by one-third. Strain. Finish with lemon juice, cream and butter.

THE FISH: Shallow poach the sole in fish stock and mushroom cooking liquor. Drain and keep warm.

Cooking the cream and eggs down with the stock has fallen out of favour, as it serves to further saturate the fats, but Langlais' mind was on other things. He ordered garnishes of prawns and mussels, lined the back with oysters and turned mushrooms, garlanded with meat glaze before adding the sauce, and then finished with truffle, diamond-shaped croûtons, gudgeon and crayfish.

Escoffier, kindly, said the truffle was perhaps optional. He took the sauce, and built on it a flight of stairs through a menu by making simple, but definite, additions and subtractions to 'create' new sauces.

RÉGENCE: Reduce a Rhine wine, fish stock with mushroom and truffle peelings, by half. Strain. Add sauce normande. Season with truffle essence.

DIPLOMAT: Season a sauce normande with lobster butter. Dice lobster meat and truffle into the sauce. Serve with large, whole fish.

RICHE: Season a sauce diplomat with black truffles and truffle essence. Serve with large whole poached fish.

VERON: Mix a sauce normande with a sauce tyrolienne (see page 65). Season with meat glaze and anchovy essence.

PARSIMONY AND SIMPLICITY

Escoffier was not beyond a joke at how simple English cooking was. Salmon poached in plain water without any seasoning at all is *à l'anglaise*. So are boiled potatoes. Compare these two recipes for a butter sauce from the *Guide*.

FRENCH: Heat flour and butter in a pan, add 1 pint water for 1oz flour. Salt. Mix 5 egg yolks, cream and lemon. Whisk this into the sauce. Heat to thicken. Strain. Finish, away from the heat, with 11oz butter.

ENGLISH: Heat 2oz butter and mix an equal amount of flour. Add 1½ pints water. Salt. Lemon. Add 7oz butter.

The English proportions are meaner: more water, less butter, no eggs or cream. The result is more parsimonious, a backdrop, as against the French sauce which sets out to aggrandize itself and its accompaniment.

English cooking at this time seems to have been content to bring its seasonings in right at the end of the process, sometimes, as with relishes and chutneys, actually on the plate itself. With French cooking, the whole process was more integrated. It worked from the inside out. One flavour was built on to another, and then grafted on to something else.

The virtues of English cooking were its simplicity and directness, the same values which, in the end, would undermine the *Guide Culinaire*.

For all its glamour, grandeur and authority, classical cooking had evolved so that it could not survive outside its chosen environment. It was a knight in shining armour, both ridiculous and splendid, but inflexible. When hotels and large houses rationalized, the cooking was cut to size. The seeds of regeneration were in more humble kitchens, back in the regions and with women's cooking.

The old cooking was also under pressure from more practical everyday problems. The hotels were working to tighter budgets. There was less space for a large brigade. The world was getting more business-like, and less leisured. Lifestyles were changing in a way that was about to influence the foods people wanted to eat. The classical kitchen trundled on like a train on a track, unable to respond by even the slightest change of direction. Sooner or later, in different parts of Europe, it came to a halt. The sell-by date elapsed.

The last gasp was perhaps the flambé restaurant, kept open by the waiters who did ninety per cent of the cooking in the dining-room, and had only one man in the kitchen to grill the steaks and make up the avocado marie-rose in the afternoon.

There was no room nor time to make the stocks, and anyway, by the early Seventies environmental health officers were actively campaigning to stamp out stock-based cookery on the grounds of health risks. Needless zealotry, but it is now law, or thereabouts, in the UK.

If there was a single point on which the door between the classic and the modern kitchen hinged, it was on the quality of the ingredients. The recipes of the classical kitchen were designed, transparently so, to compensate for any ingredient not at its best. In all probability, even nineteenth-century hotels would have struggled to find a range of high quality produce through the year. The modern kitchen was only free to go back to its regional roots on the understanding that it was working with prime produce. Otherwise, it had no pretext for what it was about to do.

POINT: THE BUILDING OF LA PYRAMIDE

FERNAND POINT (1897–1955) re-connected the monster of classical cooking to its regional roots. He brought women's cooking back into the repertory. And where the *Guide Culinaire* was able to travel anywhere in the world, Point said simply that, if you wanted to eat his food, you would have to go to him.

He was a big man, someone who made you want to sit down beside him and eat. He was an opposite to Escoffier: a country man, a restaurateur not a hotelier, a showman rather than the clerk to classical cooks. Escoffier was a little man in platform shoes, with bowler hat, brush moustache, a man of menus and form. With Point, there was no menu at all. You were asked if you wanted to eat and that was all. There was no flambéing or ceremonially serving up at the table. Dishes arrived already plated.

Point was a pyramid, and a joker. He invited the postman for a drink and had the man's bike painted yellow while he was inside; if a customer went in to the kitchen for a drink with the chef, under the chair someone would paint the heels of his shoes white. One night he took his brigade out and turned the grandstand for the next day's carnival the wrong way round. The fire brigade refused to come out to him on 1 April, and two of his rooms burned down.

His showmanship ought not to deflect from the fact that he was a serious chef. While apprenticed to the Hotel Bristol in Paris, and the Hotel Royal at Evian, he earned a reputation as a *saucier* and *pâtissier*.

THE COURTING OF CAFÉ SOCIETY

At twenty-five, he rejoined his father at the station hotel at Louhans, in the heart of the Bresse. The lease was expiring. They hoped to find a new restaurant in Lyons. The restaurant Guieu came on the market further south at Vienne.

It had a good reputation. Léon Guieu was a *traiteur* who had turned restaurateur at the end of the nineteenth century. The building was unremarkable, now another low-slung house in a wide suburban avenue, a few blocks up from the Rhône itself, and a short walk from the town centre. Vienne sells itself on its Roman ruins. Outside the restaurant, on a roundabout, is a thin, grey, needle-shaped stone pyramid, all that remains of a Roman amphitheatre around which the chariots raced. On 10 September 1923, the first stone of what was to become the restaurant La Pyramide was laid.

Point was also a businessman. Louhans was off the national road and rail links, where Vienne is on them, half-way between Paris and the Côte d'Azur. He courted Parisian café society, and they ate on their way south.

In the first years, Point contented himself with cooking Lyonnais dishes. The decor was sad, functional and low on comfort. It was his wife Marie-Louise, a hairdresser in Vienne whom he married in 1930, who brought the dynamism. She persuaded a reluctant Point to go to Paris and visit Maxim's to see what could be done. She persuaded him to close the restaurant, re-decorate, and build a second floor and a terrace on to the garden. She brought luxury. Three years later, and only seven years after the rating was introduced, La Pyramide was given three rosettes in the Michelin guide. It was an inspired move, that set a new tone for French restauration.

HIS WORKING

Point loved his Pyramide. It was his kingdom, and he rarely strayed. Even on Tuesdays, the day of closure, he invited friends in. He was generous and expansive, filling his dining room with Limoges plates and Baccarat glasses. La Pyramide stood for the re-emergence of life after the austerity of war.

Point changed his menu every day and cleared out the larder each night. The day began at five at the market. This meant he did not use stocks, not in the sense that Escoffier had. The long, integrated slabs of liquid flavour were replaced by bouillons, cooked for just two or three hours and jettisoned at the end of the day if they had not been used.

And he used butter. A lot of butter. And cream, and eggs. He judged a young chef on how he fried an egg. This was Point's way: 'Mettre du beurre dans un plat à ouefs ou une poêle, et le faire fondre à blanc (ce qui signifié qu'il faut le laisser à peine étaler, et bien entendu l'empêcher de grésiller). Casser des ouefs très frais sur une assiette plate et les faires glisser dans la poêle. C'est alors qu'il faut mettre à cuire à un feu tellement doux que le blanc d'ouef se prenne en crème, tout en veillant à ce que le jaune soit chaud. Enfin, faire fondre à part de beurre à blanc dans un casserole. Saler et poivrer légèrement, et verser au dernier moment sur les ouefs.'

Undiscovered Rhône wines, which were, after all, his local wines, underpinned his cooking. His fondue was made swaggeringly with Gruyère, Emmenthal, kirsch and the straw yellow Château Grillet, from the smallest of the main Rhône vineyards producing only 2,500 bottles a year. He deglazed the pan in which he had cooked the kidneys with a Condrieu, and then mounted a sauce with butter and cream. Both wines, interestingly, come from the little used Viognier grape.

Meals were constructed around a small number of foods – game, chicken, langoustine – each one brought to the fore. Crayfish butter was a consistent theme. He set great store by foie gras, serving it as a parfait; on a brioche; as a stuffing; unbelievably, as one dish poached in port, puréed with cream, laid on a feuilleté and topped with a poached egg.

Many of the recipes he left read as if the cooking was heavy and overly rich, but chefs who worked with him say it was light and well-judged, albeit that after the war people were hungry to taste such riches again. Point never seemed to worry as he put on more and more weight. The doctors warned him of what would happen, but he just suggested they

THE FERNAND POINT INFLUENCE

Michel Bocuse
(1765–1783)
Philibert,
Nicolas,
Jean-Noel,
Nicolas, Pierre,
Joseph, George

FERNAND POINT
(1897–1955)

Paul
Bocuse

George Blanc

La Mère Blanc

Louis Outhier

Jean-Louis Dumonet

Raymond
Thuilier

François Bise

Jean and Pierre
Troisgros

Paul Mercier

Frèdy Girardet
Bérnard Loisseau
Albert and
Michel Roux
Pierre Koffmann

Alain Chapel

Roger Vergé

Jacques Maximin
Nico Ladenis

No fewer than six three-star Michelin chefs worked in Point's kitchen. Others, like Loisseau, Girardet, Ladenis worked with and were inspired by the next generations. Curiously, the Troisgros brothers and the Roux brothers were brought up within a few miles of each other. Michel Guérard is often wrongly credited as having worked for Point. But he, like Joël Robuchon or Alain Senderens was not a direct part of the family. Girardet though, working just across the border in Crissier near Lausanne, is in the Lyons orbit of produce and had his eyes opened by doing a stage with the Troisgros brothers.

come and eat at La Pyramide, for free. 'If I stop by an unknown restaurant,' he said, 'I always ask to shake hands with the *cuisinier* before the meal. I know that if he is thin, I will eat badly.' He died, like Carême, in mid-life.

THE FOCUS CHANGES

Point is remembered as if he spoke only in short, precise epithets. The dining-room repartee follows him, via a cream notebook where he would jot down odd thoughts. Sometimes these were melancholic: 'I colour my silences with my stoves.' Or philosophic: 'Inattention never works in cooking.' Or as if talking to a pupil: 'Look at a béarnaise. What is it? An egg yolk, shallot, tarragon . . . Believe me, it takes years of practice for the result to be perfect. Take your eyes off it for a moment and your sauce will be unusable.' Or gastronomic: 'The taste of nut oils goes very well with red wine.' Or sage: 'In cuisine, you have to read everything, see everything, hear everything, try everything, observe everything to re-member, in the end, not very much . . .'

Through Point's kitchen passed an exceptional generation of young chefs. And through his dining room passed the famous: the Aga Khan, Josephine Baker, Colette, Prince Curnonksy, Jean Cocteau, General Eisenhower, the Duke and Duchess of Windsor, Edith Piaf, Rita Hay-worth, Albert Camus, Marlene Dietrich, Arthur Miller, Clark Gable etc. In the war he closed his guest book, except for one entry, for an American undercover agent who parachuted into the area and who wrote: 'I will be back in two years.' And he was.

Point shifted the focus away from Paris, and back to the heartland of French regional cookery. La Pyramide set the aspirations for the modern restaurant: large scale demonstrations of everyday culture through all the arts, from pottery to cutlery, to fabric design, to hospitality. In Paris at the turn of the century, it had been fashionable to eat after the opera, but in post-war France restaurants had to provide the drama themselves. People could not afford both. In Vienne, there was not a lot of choice.

THE MOTHERS OF LYONS

POINT'S COOKING WAS part of the Lyons dynasty. If London, thanks solely to Escoffier, was the head of the cooking, Paris the heart, then Lyons was the stomach and the sex.

The Lyons area has a strong history of restauration for good reasons. It can draw on the mountain and dairy produce of the farming communities to the east. The Rhône brings it the fish and olive oil culture of the south. And it was a trade centre, able to take lentils from Puy, chickens from Bresse, foie gras from Strasbourg, truffles from Périgord. To these same markets also came wild foods, like pike and ducks out of the Soane, frogs, snails and small birds. And there was wine on the doorstep from the Rhône and the Beaujolais. Even the Romans recognized it as a place of hospitality, and set up markets. They managed to get oysters to Lyons which, after they left, disappeared until the nineteenth century.

For similar reasons, Bath was also known for its fine food in the last century: sited at the cross roads of the drover routes; with the rich grazing pasture to the south and north; fruit and vegetables supplied on all sides; fish from the Severn and the Welsh rivers; Bristol imports from further afield. Dorothy Hartley in *Food in England* is emphatic: 'The delicious food of Bath is not only rich and elaborate, it has that perfection of simplicity which takes the very best materials, and uses them with that exquisite care which is English cooking at its best.'

Lyons has another advantage apart from being a strategic trading point. Its standing as a religious city attracted many visitors, not just to worship, but also to politic. The spiritual interpretation is that the table is the place where family and friends gather for grace and to break bread and, as such, is the focal point of the pious day. Therefore, there ought to be no obstacle to enjoying the foods available. Piety and eroticism are said to be the twin passions of the Lyonnais soul.

CUISINE BOURGEOIS

Unlike in Paris, where professional cooks congregated after the revolution, in Lyons it was the women who took on the role. Here was a cooking of a different style altogether, born out of the market, largely domestic and individual, and centred not on the luxuries of the classical kitchen, but on the inexpensive trimmings from the butchers' tables. Nor was there any talk of inventing dishes. These were recipes that had been handed down through generations, and had been honed to sharpness.

The gratin here was elevated to civic status. Felix Benoit, the city's gastronomic biographer, gives this rather over-the-top variation as the traditional way.

LA GRATINÉE LYONNAIS

FOR 4: Take 300g Gruyère. Grate half. Slice the rest thinly. Put a little of the grated cheese, with some butter, in the bottom of a soup bowl. Grill 3 slices of thin bread. Lay them in the soup bowl covering the first with slices of cheese, the second with the grated and the top with the last of the slices. Pour over this a bouillon of burnt onions. Season. Put in the oven until all the bouillon is soaked up by the bread. Fill the bowl with more bouillon, pepper and half a glass of cognac. Cook on for 5 minutes. Before serving, pour over an egg whipped in port. Serve very hot.

THE PIG'S EARS

The *charcutiers* of Lyons worked not just with pigs, but with offal from all the farmyard animals. At the Léon de Lyon in the narrow Rue Pleney, so tight that the restaurant can only be photographed side on, the menu still carries on, at least in part, the rich tradition which owes perhaps as much to the east of France, as does the wooden aubergiste decor inside:

Gras double émincé, confit avec oignons, tomates, vin blanc, puis gratiné 88fr

Lyonnaiseries en salade: Pied d'agneau, pied de veau émincé, cervelas, museau, boudin cru, pâté de tête et sabodet (saucisson cuit de couenne), servies avec un cake tiède aux oreilles de cochon 87 fr

Salade d'herbes crues (cerfeuil, ciboulette, estragon, oseille, persil simple, épinard, cresson) aux langues d'agneau confites, vinaigrette au jus d'agneau, pain toaste aux herbes 82 fr

Pied de porc désossé puis remis dans une farce fine, oreille de cochon panée puis poêlée, cuisson au persil simple tres légèrement moutardée, garniture de saison 99 fr

Gâteau de foies de volaille, sauce suprême liée au foie gras, garni de crêtes, rognons de coq et petit quenelles de volaille 100 fr

The offcuts have been raised to a gastronomic tourist draw.

But it is perhaps the sausage for which Lyons is best known. This recipe comes from Roger Roucou, who is one of the father figures of modern French gastronomy and who carries on at La Mère Guy, which dates back to 1759 and was one of the first eating houses to be opened by a

SEETHE HITWITH AN ESY FIRE . . .'

woman. There have been many mères Guys since, including the most respected, La Génie, around 1870, who claimed to be English. But the founding mother might be surprised to find it in its present form, under Roger Roucou on the banks of the Soane, because she was there before the re-planning of the waterways, when it was on the Rhône.

The sausage survives on a menu that otherwise deals in classical cooking, with much foie gras. It is served with boiled potatoes. There are two Lyons sausages, one similar to those found in other regions of France and this one, known more commonly as a cervelas, and seasoned with truffle and pistachio. It is properly a *charcutier's* dish because it needs a *charcutier's* stove, an *étuve*. This is the recipe, as it hangs in the kitchen of La Mère Guy.

SAUCISSON LYONNAIS AFTER ROGER ROUCOU

Ingredients	350g red meat
	350g fresh breast, skinned and boned
	300g fat from the neck or throat
	or
	750g red meat
	250g fat from the neck or throat
	30g cooked, chopped truffle
	10g truffle cooked in the round
	12–15g whole pistachios
Salt cure	20–24g salt
	2g sugar
	1g saltpetre
Seasoning	1.5g powdered grey pepper
	1.5g grey peppercorns
	1g grated nutmeg
	3cl cognac, port or Madeira
Liaison	10g dairy starter culture
Wrapping	Skins

PROGRESS OF WORK

– Put the red meat and the neck fat in the salt. Minimum 12 hours.
– Wash the skins in cold water.
– Rinse (smooth side outside).
– Grind the pistachios.
– Prepare the seasoning, the liaison and the chopped truffle.
– Mix the meat and the fat.
– Put in the mixer.

– Add the seasoning, the liaison, chopped truffle and crushed pistachios.
– Add the cognac, port or madeira.
– Mix to effect the liaison.
– Fill a cloth that you will use as the squeeze bag, making sure there are no pockets of air.
– Put four or five rounds of truffle on the nozzle.
– Cut a piece of skin about 20cm long and string the end.
– Turn back the skin.
– Roll the skin over the nozzle without dislodging the truffles.
– Stuff carefully.
– Tie up, leaving one string for hanging.
– Hang to strain and dry.
– Etuver for a good colour (about 20 minutes).

FIVE DISHES

Point's mother was a well-known cook. He re-introduced women's cooking, that had been languishing in the backstreets and garrets, to the repertoire. His gastronomic family were the mothers Bigot, Pompou, Coquit, Carton, Guy, Fillioux, Genot, Lea, and Michel who cooked, it was said, like other women made love. One mother even took her stock to bed in a jar to keep her warm.

The best known was Françoise Fayolle at La Mère Fillioux, 73 Rue Duquesne, who turned a workers' café into a national monument at the beginning of this century. 'The making of a dish takes years of experience. I spent all my life doing four or five dishes, so now I know how to do them, I do not do anything else.' Those five dishes were *potage velouté aux truffes*; *quenelles au gratin au beurre d'écrevisses*; *cuisses d'artichaut au foie gras*; *volaille demi-deuil* and, to be ordered in advance, *langouste à l'américaine*.

Demi-deuil, ie half-mourning, is achieved by the white skin and black truffle. The chicken was from Bresse, gutted to leave the head on, the sliced truffles slipped beneath the skin, the bird wrapped in a muslin, plunged into a chicken consommé, brought to the boil and simmered gently for twenty minutes (Bresse chickens are not as thick fleshed as other birds); served garnished with carrots, potatoes, gherkins, coarse salt and mustard.

THE CÔTE D'OR

Point, and the others who worked with him, picked up this tradition of female cookery. He was not alone. André Pic at Le Pin, near Valence, was probably his equal as a technician. His maxims were to cook to order, to make sauces at the last minute, and to use the best produce. Alexandre Dumaine, at the Côte d'Or at Saulieu, was almost as well known in the Thirties and achieved fame without the backing of Lyons.

The Côte d'Or carries on as a great restaurant under Bérnard Loisseau, and Dumaine's very bourgeois dining room is still used. The large square room is filled with mahogany beams – single struts across the ceiling interspersed with thin red planking – and padding around windows and doors. Occasionally, the pistachio of the walls breaks in, but it is mostly covered with friezes in the same mauve as the tablecloths. Mirrors on the backs of the doors create an illusion of being in a painting. Even the flowers, one vase per table plus a major display at the door, could be still life, which in a way is how Dumaine would have wanted it to be. Here, he cooked dishes like a *ragoût* of crayfish, cooked in a *mirepoix*, layered in a gratin dish with truffles, speckled with cheese and gratinated. Or a Bresse chicken, truffled, and marinated in Marsala, steamed in a large earthen-ware pot which was brought out and only opened at table, so the aroma of truffles exploded into the whole room. For another dinner, he served a *pot-au-feu* as four courses: first the beef, then a chicken, then a ham and finally a sausage.

LES BONNES TABLES

Michelin's three-starred restaurants in 1935 with their credited specialities.

CÔTE D'OR

Saulieu, Côte d'Or
(Jambon de Morvan à la creme;
truite et écrevisses au Montrachet,
poularde des ducs de Bourgogne)

FOYOT

Paris 6th
(Homard Foyot, poulet Foyot;
crêpes flambées)

LAPÉROUSE

Paris 6th
(Caneton nantais Colette; homard
Lapérouse; champignons
Lapérouse)

TOUR D'ARGENT

Paris 5th
(Croustade de barbue Lagrene;
fillets de sole Cardinal; caneton)

CHÂTEAU JACQUES COEUR

Boisy, Loire
(Vol au vent d'écrevisses; potée
forézienne flanquée de perdreaux;
pintadeau au Calvados)

CHEZ LA MÈRE BRAZIER

Col de la Luere, Rhône
(Quennelles au gratin, volaille
Mére Brazier, langouste Belle
Aurore)

LUCAS CARTON
Paris 8th
(Sole de ma Tante Marie; gratin de homard Lucas; becasse flambée)

LARUE
Paris 8th
(No specialities listed)

CAFÉ DE PARIS
Paris 2nd
(No specialities listed)

EUROPE ET ANGLETERRE
Mâcon, Saône
(Pâté maison, foie gras, homard à l'americaine)

FRANCE
Moosch, Haut Rhin
(Truite au bleu; écrevisses; poularde aux morilles)

CHAPON FIN
Bordeaux, Gironde
(Fillets de sole Chapon Fin; Tournedos Diplomate; crêpes à la Bordelaise)

MÈRE BRAZIER
Lyons, Rhône
(Quennelles au gratin, volaille demi-deuil; crêpes au curaçao)

LA PYRAMIDE
Vienne, Isère
(Gratin de queues d'écrevisses; truite farcie braisée au porto; poularde en vessie)

MIDI
Lamastre, Ardeche
(Pâté de canard, pain d'écrevisses, poularde à l'ancienne)

PIC
St Peray, Cevennes
(Gratin de queues d'écrevisses, poule en vessie; boudin Richelieu sauce écrevisses)

BOURGEOIS
Priay, Ain
(Pâté chaud, gratin de queues d'écrevisses, truite meunière)

Only seventeen restaurants earned the denotation as *une des meilleures tables de France, vaut le voyage.* North and south were almost completely ignored. Paris and an area within 100 kilometres radius of Lyons contribute 14 of the addresses. Ecrevisses were the flavour of the year. Note the similarities between Point's specialities and Pic's.

Opposite: Page 601 of the Michelin guide in 1935 revealed the extraordinary powerhouse of Lyons restaurants – 19 restaurants listed sharing 31 stars.

Sauf indication contraire, voir emplacements sur plan ci-contre.

XXX❋❋ **Albert Renault**, 14 r. Grolée, l 13-3, Rep 20/30 ☏ Franklin **71.60**. Spéc. :
Écrevisses en gelée − Menu à 30 fr : Feuilleté de morilles, Poulet sauté lyonnaise − Clos de la Pucelle,
Châteauneuf-du-Pape Clos Papal 1923.

XXX❋❋ **Morateur**, r. St-Bonaventure, h 13-3, Rep 25/35 ☏ Franklin **36.76**. Spéc. :
Entrecôte Morateur − Menu à 35 fr : Timbale de queues d'écrevisses, Gratin du chanoine − Marétel des
Altesses, Musigny de Vogué 1904-1911.

XXX❋❋❋ **Mère Brazier**, 12 r. Royale, w 13-2, Rep 30/40 ☏ Burdeau **15.49**. Spéc. :
Quenelles au gratin, Volaille demi-deuil − Menu à 40 fr : Crêpes au curaçao − Châteauneuf-du-Pape.

XX❋❋ **Sorret**, 24 quai Retz, f 13-3, Rep à la carte ☏ Franklin **45.72**. Spéc. : Avec suppl¹ :
Langouste belle Aurore, Truite braisée au porto, Volaille Nantua − Richebourg 1911, Château-Yquem.

XX❋❋ **Mère Fillioux**, 73 r. Duquesne, d 14-2, plan en couleurs, Rep 35 ☏ La-
lande **3.19**. Spéc. : Volaille truffée demi-deuil, Quenelles au gratin au beurre d'écrevisses, Fonds d'arti-
chauts au foie gras truffé − Châteauneuf-du-Pape 1926, Fleurie 1929.

XX❋❋ **Mère Guy**, 35 quai J.-J.-Rousseau, e 11-6, plan en couleurs, Rep 35 et à la carte
☏ Franklin **8.41**. Spéc. : Matelote « Mère Guy », Brochetons éclusière, Volaille villageoise − Condrieux.

XX❋❋ **Garcin**, 11 r. Algérie, a 12-2, Rep 25/35 ☏ Burdeau **18.58**. Spéc. : Quenelles
maison − Avec suppl¹ : Brochetons éclusière, Gratin de queues d'écrevisses − Corton Charlemagne.

XX❋ **Farge**, 1 pl. Cordeliers, g 13-3, Rep 30 et à la carte ☏ Franklin **37.64**. Spéc. :
Gras-double lyonnaise, Volaille demi-deuil − Quenelles au gratin − Morgon, Moulin-à-Vent.

XX❋❋ **Surgère**, 10 r. Confort, o 13-3, Rep à la carte ☏ Franklin **34.57**. Spéc. : Sur comm. :
Gratin d'écrevisses, Filet de sole maison, Poulet Brillat-Savarin.

XX❋❋ **Francotte** (fermé dim et fêtes de la Pentecôte au 20 sept.), 8 pl. Célestins, t 12-3.
Rep à la carte ☏ Franklin **38.64**. Spéc. : Sur comm. : Langouste à la crème, Rouget grillé, Râble de
lièvre à la crème.

XX❋❋ **Filet de Sole**, 34 r. Ferrandière, j 13-3, Rep 20/25 ☏ Franklin **44.06**. Spéc. :
Quenelles lyonnaise − Menu à 25 fr : Filets de sole maison − Avec suppl¹ : Poulet hongroise − Moulin-à-Vent
1929, Richebourg 1929.

XX❋ **Rivier**, 1 pl. Terreaux, b 13-2, Rep à la carte ☏ Burdeau **2.35**. Spéc. : Vins : Hospices-
de-Beaune 1923, Moulin-à-Vent 1929.

XX❋ **Café Neuf (Vettard)**, 7 pl. Bellecour, q 13-3, Rep 22/30, dim 25/30 ☏ Franklin
7.59. Spéc. : Filet de marcassin, Sole au gratin, Quenelles « Café Neuf » − Brouilly, Meursault.

X❋❋ Mme Léon Déan (Le Capitole), 22 boul. Brotteaux, Rep 20 (bc). à la carte, dim
22 (bc). à la carte ☏ Lalande **76.47**. Spéc. : A la carte : Champignons farcis, Coq au vin, Langouste
au gratin − Vouvray, Châteauneuf-du-Pape.

X❋ Vignard Joseph « Chez Juliette » (fermé le dim de Pâques à fin sept.), 23 r. Arbre-
Sec, y 13-2, Rep à la carte ☏ Burdeau **64.06**. Spéc. : Rognons maison, Volaille à la crème, Langouste
maison − Brouilly, Viré clos de la Roche.

X❋ Renaissance Martin Buisson, 7-9 r. Childebert, n 13-3, ☏ Franklin **19.52**.

X❋❋ Lamour, 19 pl. Tolozan, c 13-2, Rep à la carte ☏ Burdeau **35.77**. Spéc. : Chausson
aux queues d'écrevisses, Coq au vin.

X Tony, 26 quai Retz, i 13-3, Rep 10/15 ☏ Franklin **3.28**.

X❋ Chateaubriand (Thibaud), 3 pl. Kléber, u 14-2, plan en couleurs, Rep 15/20
☏ Lalande **63.83**. Spéc. : Avec suppl¹ : Quenelles de brochet au four, Grenouilles à la Batellière − Sur
comm. et avec suppl¹ : Coq de Bresse au Chambertin.

Au Mont-Ceindre (N : 9 k.) - ✉ ⚲ ☏ à St-Cyr-au-Mont-d'Or :
X **Bellevue**, ⚑, Rep 3. 17/20. 12/15, dim 20. 15/17 − Ch 12 à 15 (16ch) Abri (5) grat
⚑ ☏ 0.28.

PLANS EN COULEURS FIN DU GUIDE

**Si, à LYON, le fournisseur de pneus auquel vous vous adressez n'a
pas l'article dont vous avez besoin, demandez-lui de se le procurer
sans délai à l'ENTREPOT MICHELIN de Lyon.**

MICHELIN et Cⁱᵉ, Entrepôt (VENTE EN GROS ; Renseign.), 167 r. Vendôme (3ᵉ) (14-3).
Entrée des Mag. : 8 r. Le-Royer (3ᵉ) (14-3). ⚲ Pneumiclin Lyon ☏ Moncey 575.

Voir emplacements sur plan page suivante.

1ᵉʳ Arrondissement.

STOCK MICHELIN **Gar. de la Martinière**, 33 pl. Martinière, 12-2, ☏ Burdeau 19.13 et 64.68.
STOCK MICHELIN **Gar. de la Soierie**, Ambre et Fauvet, 10 r. Capucins, j 13-2, ☏ Bur-
deau 20.25. . . . . **DELAUNAY.**
🏁 Gar. St-Vincent, 32 et 35 quai St-Vincent, ☏ Burdeau 01.72 et 18.30.
⚓ Demal, 19 quai St-Vincent, ☏ Burdeau 20.80.

(Voir fin du texte p. 603 à 605.)

THE NEW MASTERS

The dynasty that traces its roots back to the mothers of Lyons now dominates French cooking. Even those who were not actually part of the Lyonnais tradition itself, pay homage. Paul Bocuse, the Troisgros brothers, Georges Blanc, Alain Chapel, Louis Outhier, all worked for Point himself. Others, like Frédy Girardet at Crissier, still work in the influence of that market. Without Lyons there would be hardly any three-star Michelin, or 19/20-plus in *Gault-Millau*. The *Guide Culinaire*, in guide book terms, was finally routed in the Sixties and Seventies.

The markets of Lyons are not what they were, and the reputation of the restaurants is rather fanciful. Both Elizabeth David and Waverley Root, writing in the Fifties, record their sense of disappointment, finding a cooking that lacked the finesse of other regions and leaned rather too heavily on the bludgeoning habits of middle-European cooking. The exceptions seem the greater because of the general lacklustre that has taken over, as if Lyonnais cooking has once again moved back into the home. The cold hand of modern agro business has been tugging at the city's hem. Many of the chefs now have their produce delivered from Rungis, outside Paris. No longer is it easy for a chef to find a ready set up market nearby, that can supply on a regular basis with the kind of quality customers and he have come to expect.

BOCUSE:
THE MAIN STREAM

PAUL BOCUSE INHERITED the Lyonnais traditions. Michel Bocuse, a fisherman, duck-catcher and occasional pirate on the Soane, opened a small *cabaret* for workers and the bourgeois in 1765. It sold *fritures* – fish and chips.

The restaurant stands on the same site at Collonges au Mont d'Or, a short drive along the river out of Lyons on the merciless one-way system. The square building is painted a deep, bright red with oriental temple trimmings, splashes of green, the ten letters that spell Paul Bocuse stretched out in neon across the front of the building. Little plaques in the stonework commemorate how high the floods came in different years when the river burst its bank. To the side is a car park the size of a motor-way service area. There are four dining-rooms, and 150 covers are served per night. Every night. Sixty people are employed full-time.

The menu bears a bizarre collage of a Fifties black-and-white dining-room scene: two businessmen chat, while their raven-haired, multi-pearled companion with the cleavage toasts the chef, Bocuse himself, implanted in full colour, clad in his chef's whites. He is bearing the seabass *en croute* on a silver salver and looking like a French John Wayne. Underneath, the caption says deliberately, *Cuisine de Tradition*.

And that is what it is today, a country cooking raised to a classical state, neither totally traditional nor ultra-modern, but steadily down the main stream of French cooking.

A few linchpin pieces of showmanship provide the axis: the same seabass *en croute* as shown on the menu, shaped and re-made so the pastry is a dark brown sculpture of the fish itself which can be opened at table; the chicken *en vessie*, that springs out of its bladder to be carved, also at table; the delicate scaling of sauté potatoes down the back of the red mullet; the truffle soup encased in pastry, referred to in shorthand as VGE, and created for Valéry Giscard d'Estaing in 1975, when d'Estaing came to Lyons to pin the *Légion d'honneur* on Bocuse. The sweet course is a comedian going through a well-worn but successful gag: just a few chocolate truffles and pastries arrive, as if to accompany coffee, and then a perfect crème caramel, the restraint seems admirable, but finally, after everyone thought they had finished, comes the climax of trollies of bowls filled with fruits, sorbets, more sweets, more pastries, glasses of fruits macerated in wine. The restaurant has become opera.

THE ROW OVER NOUVELLE CUISINE

Conservative estimates put the turnover at more than £7.5 million a year. How much it brings France in foreign currency, is anybody's guess. It is the clearest, and most definite statement, that 'the best restaurant in the world' can exist. Bocuse himself has taken the ambassadorial lead from Carême, and opened businesses in Orlando, Hong Kong and Japan, but none of this has fully rubbed off. Listening to him, you still feel you are occupying space usually reserved for the apprentice. The tone is conciliatory, but the convictions are immovable and combative. He is, as the French say, *sérieux*.

He fought and was injured in the free French army in the war, and still refers to his English apprentices as improving because they have short hair. This makes them serious, too, ready for a day's work. I asked him how he judged a young chef. Not through his cooking, he said, because he could teach him that. What he looked for was the boy in the schoolyard who picked up the scrap of litter. Someone who spotted the smaller details. '*I have often been called the father of this* nouvelle cuisine, *quite wrongly, because my interpretation is completely different. I have always denounced this revolution as being more about men, than about food. We discover, across the world, since* nouvelle cuisine, *an alarming culinary uniformity. The mini carrot beside a tiny turnip, accompanied by a pea cut in four, the whole lot supporting an emaciated fillet of a bird from which the skin and bones have been taken, or a steamed fish with a timbale of vegetables collapsed into a purée. This works on the level of colour, but to the detriment of taste. The eye is flattered, but not the other senses. It is a cuisine for people who have lost their appetites, and are becoming anorexic. Worse, this ethereal food is served jealously guarded under cloches, in case it might fly off between the kitchen and the dining room.*

'*It is a light cooking, the only thing difficult to digest is the bill, which sits heavily on the stomach: the more deserted the plate, the more lavish the bill. I have travelled the world, and it revolts me to see the same dish served in every country I visit. Every country has its cooking, each region its specialities. I cannot imagine going to Spain, for example, without tasting a paella, or eating one of their farmhouse hams washed down with a glass of Rioja. It is part of travelling. Food helps one to understand the culture and traditions of an area.*

'*You do not invent in cooking. You adjust. You adapt. You interpret to a point, but that is all. We have to be realistic and modest, and, to make sure that we are not mistaken, ensure that we use the best produce of the season. Today you can find foods in season through the year, but do not tell me that to serve strawberries at Christmas, from the other end of the world, is anything but heresy. They are hard as wood, and taste of the grave. Where is the aroma? It is time to denounce this system, and find a more substantial cuisine where all the senses can come into play. The cuisinier who can marry a little of the excesses of yesterday with the best products of the day will succeed.*

'*The foods deserve respect, and should be treated with diffidence. Be careful of too many subtle tricks, because the table is a refuge where a man can recharge himself. Try and concoct a style of cooking that will warm his heart again.*

'*My definition of* nouvelle cuisine *comes from Fernand Point. He was the first to give the table a new look. He was the detonator. He gave cooking and the dining-room the atmosphere of the festival. It was a time after the war, when everyone was hungry for rich and filling foods. No one knew of calories. Butter, cream, wine were our credo, used without restraint.*

'Previously, famous chefs had always been employed in the big houses where the patron was a banker, or a businessman, or a hotelier. These chefs headed brigades, often impressively large brigades, but they lived their lives in the basement, rarely seeing the sun. This is where the real revolution took place. Chefs took it on themselves to run their profession by opening their own restaurants. A new politic arose. The chef did his own shopping, became responsible for the well-being of his own business, but above all he came into direct contact with his customers.'

Brigade chefs had the buying done for them. For the classical hotel chef, cooking was a self-contained skill. Produce was something that came from somewhere else, and was there to be dominated. The idea of using it as a guide to how to cook, was absurd. That was something that happened in homes, something women did.

THE IMPORTANCE OF THE PRODUCE

But the shopping itself, if overtly just a means of quality control, taught an awareness of different foods, of the seasons, of varieties and species. From this grew another philosophy: that the optimum was simply to get something to taste of itself. Anything else was just playing games.

It is easy now to overlook how much of a breakthrough this idea seemed at the time. The difference, was the boundary of responsibility. The domain of the classical kitchen stretched only as far as the kitchen walls. To the modern kitchen it could stretch, if need be, right out to the market garden.

Alice Waters, of the modest but exact Chez Panisse in Berkeley, California, catches the sense of discovery: 'In that little restaurant I went to in Brittany, they caught the fish in the stream, and they pulled the oysters right out of the whatever. The best mussels I ever had, right at the port. They brought the mussels in and dunked them in this pot. I will never forget it. And they brought a big bowl to the table, and you ate until you were full. Now, I was always wondering, why do they taste so good? And when I came back (to America) I tried to cook mussels, but they never tasted that way. It wasn't until we went out to the beach right here one day, and brought the oysters in. We opened them up. And I must have eaten about four dozen. It hit like a light bulb. It's because they are just out of the water.'

As with Escoffier's stocks, this was a thought that could leap borders. And if the produce was good and fresh enough it could, as the Japanese had shown, compete with any number of skills invoked by a whole brigade of classical chefs.

NOT SO NOUVELLE

So much has been written and said about so-called *nouvelle cuisine*, that it has been talked into something that it never was. There have been *nouvelle cuisines* since before Carême (and there have been books on *Modern Cooking*: as I write, I am looking at a 1955 version replete with Cornish Heavy Cake, Dripping Cake, Eggless Cake, Fruit Soda Cake). But in 1972, when Henri Gault and Christian Millau launched their new guide to restaurants in France, a new cooking or, at least, a new style, was obvious and demonstrable.

Amid the chi-chi, could be found the crucial tenets on which the cooking had turned. *Nouvelle cuisine* was a point on a line, the first visible symptom of a more exaggerated process that is still carrying on. At its best it is, as Jacques Maximin said, what happens when a skilled *cuisinier* confronts a new area, new suppliers, new foods and new ideas, which is all Escoffier did when he came north from Provence. '*I loved the Nicois region, before I loved its cooking. Then, seeking a culinary identity, I looked more closely at the vast reservoir of good produce this countryside offers, and I soon realised that it was on that which I must rely. I had to find out how to resuscitate, research, reform, or simply re-think this cuisine right from its roots, to prove that the Nicois region was not just a gastronomic backwater.*'

OTHER INFLUENCES

Nouvelle cuisine marked a point where the French kitchen had finally let in other influences, especially from the east. Escoffier's world had encompassed Naples to the south, Hungary to the east, Biarritz to the west, Scotland to the north. The global village brought seasonings from Thailand and India; precision and abstraction from Japan; and, perhaps most important of all, an understanding of textures such as was found in Hong Kong and the Canton.

The classical kitchen had taken little notice of textures. The final dish was often a composition, in which the different elements had been deliberately re-fashioned into mousses and stuffings so their origins were obscure. Flour in the sauces served to flatten them out.

This point is important in explaining why things came to change, why there was a need for more than a couple of elements on a plate, why some foods were brought into play with others, and why there was pressure on a *cuisinier*, like a golfer, to use a range of different skills.

For the Chinese kitchen, textures are critical. Pork fat gives gelatinousness to a stew. Chicken feet flavoured with star anise, are chewed for their fibrousness. Intestines are prized for their smoothness and resilience. In European cookery, outside Lyons, such parts of the animal were consigned to different fates: the fat to melt down as a cooking medium, the chicken feet to stock, the intestines to sausages.

The Chinese sense of relationships between flavours and objects was inspirational: yin being cold, negative, gentle as represented by the moon, the female, darkness, weakness; yang being hot, positive, aggressive and represented by the sun, the male, light, strength. The ideal was balance. Red meats are yang, fish is yin. Here, symbolically, was a form of codification for the sort of harmonies between different ingredients and flavours that the kitchen was seeking. Even if it did not believe in them, there was a blueprint that could be followed. Here was something Escoffier had not written about.

Going further east to Japan, there was a similar blueprint available, this time making use of the different cooking techniques to provide contrast through a meal of many different courses: simmer, grill, boil, raw, cooked, shallow fry, deep fry, pickle.

INNOCENT VANITIES

There was more than an element of cause and effect about the whole battered phenomenon of *nouvelle cuisine*.

Putting the sauce under the fish or meat meant the main attraction was not hidden. Inevitably, the result was more designered dishes. The packaging had been thrown away.

Taking the flour out of the sauces – all four of Escoffier's favoured quartet of stocks and sauces contained flour – lightened the cooking, because they were not laden with the butter needed to absorb the flour in the first place.

The small portions were an innocent vanity, the kitchen a bit dazzled at what it was seeing, and anxiously feeling its way for a new balance.

Cutting the cooking times right back so that vegetables are firm to the bite, lamb cooked pink, fish heated until the flesh just blushes and the sinews let go their hold on the bones, meant much more could be done to order. The classical kitchen had been geared up to pre-preparation. Menus came down to the size of the kitchen.

Another fundamental departure was probably necessary, as a process through which the kitchen could learn and reappraise, but is unconvincing in itself. In both classical and regional cooking, meats and fish are cooked for preference on the bone. Fillets on a large fish were cut horizontally for that very reason. The new cooking demanded that flesh and carcass be separated, and prepared apart. The creative work went into the sauce. Fillets were cooked simply. For fish, they were cut lengthways. The sauce took over centre stage, which had been one of the charges levelled at the classical kitchen.

The cooking opened up. If a cake, in the classical and regional interpretation, was a single block containing all its different components; the modern kitchen set out to dismantle the whole idea. Spread out across the plate were a slice of sponge, a fruit, a syrup, a garnish, a bit of cream.

Looking back to 1972, the picture is of a two-dimensional cooking: meat and sauce, two colours starkly laid out on a plate. Mono before stereo.

Since that time, the cooking might be said to have reached puberty and filled out. More items appear on the plate. The look is less minimalist, more revivalist, rich in textures and colours. At its best, it is a deliberate bringing together of tastes, using prime produce according to the season, and setting it off for contrasts of textures, flavours and colours.

And, as with the mothers of Lyons, it is once again a very personal and individual cooking.

BREATHS
OF
MOVEMENT

—

FISH COOKING

THE DAM BEHIND which the classical cooking had swelled for the best part of 100 years, finally burst at fish. The hot cooking was based on texturous, sinuous amalgamations of flour and butter; the cold on transparent, gelatinous aspics. Fish cooking was an older and weaker side of the classical craft, more committed to the idea of disguise. Fillets went through make-up rather than cookery – dusted in flour, wiped in breadcrumbs, smeared through batters, greased with butter, pan-fried, shallow-fried – the wonder was that the species in the middle could be identified at all. Poached fish was no sooner done, than it was taken out of the liquid and shoved back into the oven to dry out, while the kitchen began work on the important business, its overcoat and galoshes.

The bulk of the recipes in the *Guide Culinaire* were slanted towards a few types of fish: sole and turbot for white; lobster for crustacea; salmon for river fish. Their ascendancy was supreme. Other fish, like plaice or lemon sole, were too thin to survive such treatments. The thicker fleshed, meatier fish did not attract the same enthusiasm. Monkfish is mentioned, only to be dismissed: 'Not considered to be of much value except for the reputation of its liver; this is prepared in the same way as soft roes, bearing in mind that it takes a little longer to cook.' There are, on the other hand, eighty-two recipes for sole.

Such dependence on individual fish led inevitably to the price rising to the point that the modern kitchen looked elsewhere. Brill, monk, John Dory, red mullet, skate, seabass, whiting, scallops, even cod were welcomed back into the repertoire. They were cheaper, and presented a new creative agenda.

THE HOLLANDAISE FAMILY

The work changed, too. Instead of tending the rolling stockpots, now the chef was a specialist. He traded four or five big vats for a line of small copper saucepans, a ladle for a whisk. The modern chef worked hunched over a flame, beating out an emulsification.

One classical sauce family translated gloriously into *nouvelle cuisine* The hollandaise. From this side of the *Guide Culinaire*, the modern kitchen evolved its style of saucing.

The hollandaise is French, and arrived in England after its Siamese twin, the mayonnaise. At first glance, this timing seems strange, because oil had to be imported, where English butter was excellent. There is a thesis that this reflects the underlying differences in attitudes. British butter sauces were invariably thickened with flour, as part of a wider investment in baking. The French took the cockerel as their national symbol, and eggs were part of the cooking because they were central to a way of life.

There are more tangible and persuasive reasons: the lush grazing of English downlands produced salted sweetcream butters, rather than the lactics of north Europe. Vinegars were malted, rather than wine. Lemon was an expensive import. The ingredients were not native. A cynic might add that the hollandaise is not an easy sauce.

INTENSE ESSENCES

The butter has to be added slowly, small pieces at a time, to give the yolks time to absorb the fat. Heat arrests the process. If it is too hot, the result is simply scrambled eggs.

The technique is the shape of an egg-timer. A wide-flavoured liquid is reduced down to the narrowest, most intense of essences, then built up into almost the same volume again, only by this time it has been transformed into something completely different. The sauce repays using delicate, good quality ingredients. The water can be replaced with stock, wine or cooking juices; the vinegar flavoured with herbs or reinforced with lemon juice. The reduction builds up the acidity.

BASIC HOLLANDAISE AFTER THE GUIDE
CULINAIRE

STAGE 1: Reduce 4 tablespoons of water to 2 of vinegar by two-thirds. Set aside in a bain-marie to cool.

STAGE 2: Beat 5 egg yolks with a little water. Add to the vinegar reduction. Return to a low heat.

STAGE 3: Cut 1 lb of butter into small cubes (or heat it separately to a liquid). Whisk one piece vigorously into the reduction and yolks. Add the next, whisking all the time so each fragment of butter is absorbed before the next is added. Add a few drops of water if the sauce looks too thick. Season with salt. Add a squeeze of lemon.

Carême suggested using a little meat or fish glaze to stabilize. Other cooks use cream. The final sauce ought to be, to use the cliché which was probably invented for it, thick enough to coat the back of a spoon, viscous with some body. The lemon juice adds further acidity.

The addition of other flavours creates other sauces: blood oranges for a Maltaise; thick cream for Chantilly or a mousseline. Classically, the sauce was laid over the fish and glazed under the grill before serving. The modern kitchen puts the fish on the sauce.

TWO SIDES OF THE FAMILY

The hollandaise are a cosmopolitan family, taking in hard, peasant-proven regional recipes on one side, and on the other appearing at royal tables. The two sides split between oil and butter.

THE HOLLANDAISE FAMILY

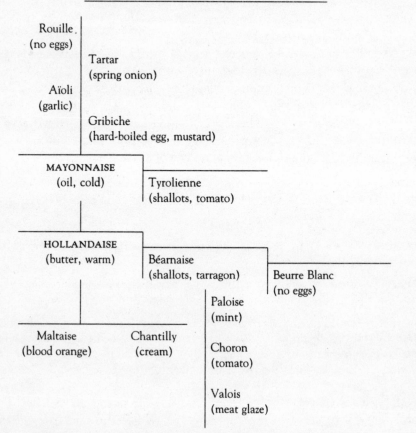

Rouille
(no eggs)

Tartar
(spring onion)

Aïoli
(garlic)

Gribiche
(hard-boiled egg, mustard)

MAYONNAISE
(oil, cold)

Tyrolienne
(shallots, tomato)

HOLLANDAISE
(butter, warm)

Béarnaise
(shallots, tarragon)

Beurre Blanc
(no eggs)

Paloise
(mint)

Maltaise
(blood orange)

Chantilly
(cream)

Choron
(tomato)

Valois
(meat glaze)

For mayonnaise, oil replaces butter and the initial reduction is dropped, although some cooks use a little mustard to season the base, which performs the same role. Otherwise, it is the same slow amalgamation of fluid into egg yolk, the same stiffening of texture, the same ability to show off other flavours, especially herbs. The oil base is universally used for cold sauces, the butter for hot. The one is a southern sauce, or at least a summer one; the other, northern.

The mayonnaise and its descendants are more closely identifiable with rural cooking. That side of the family has more to do with ingredients than with techniques, although not in the way that they are eventually used. Aïoli takes a mayonnaise through all the same stages as the hollandaise.

AÏOLI

STAGE 1: Skin some garlic cloves. Boil in 2 changes of water (to take away the bitter fieriness of Provençal garlic). Purée.

STAGE 2: Beat in the yolks of 2 hard-boiled eggs and 2 raw egg yolks.

STAGE 3: Whisk 7 fl oz olive oil, starting a dribble a time, and building up to a thin line. Season.

The use of aïoli as part of a bourride, is a potent statement about the quality of French cooking at the southern ports. The aïoli mixes with the stock to thicken and flavour, and turns a fish gratin into something dramatic.

BOURRIDE

THE SOUP: Stew garlic, fennel, red pepper, onions in oil until soft, but not coloured. Add 6lb white Mediterranean fish to 3½ pints water. Bring to a boil. Season. Add a live crawfish. Simmer 15 minutes. Remove crawfish and split.

THE SAUCE: Strain the stock through a sieve on to the aïoli, beating continuously to amalgamate. Lay bread in bowls, and spread with more aïoli. Ladle the stock over the croûtons. Serve the fish separately, with more aïoli to the side.

Aïoli and rouille have, mistakenly, come to be seen as interchangeable, probably because both are intrinsic parts of Provençal soups. But the rouille has no eggs, so its kinship is more distant, where the aïoli is obviously a blood relation. There is a thought that the aïoli is a sauce from inland, where people would keep chickens and buy their fish from markets; while the rouille was an urban port compromise, which does without the egg which could cost extra. Rouille developed along with the bouillabaise, which was made with the sort of fish more likely to be found on the shoreline and, in part at least, fished by the family. Original versions left the bones in, which with the small inshore marauders, made it a bony meal.

THE BOUILLABAISSE

Bouillabaisse must be among the most eloquent of dishes that speak for a region of the world. The whole geography of coastal Provence seems to be wound up in it: the heat, the smells, the wet, the reds and ochres, the scant stubble of green are all there. At more expensive restaurants, the serving has been elevated to ritual.

At Baçon in boulevard Baçon at Cap d'Antibes, the waiters tie large bibs around diners, before filleting the spiny rascasse, weever, galinette, baudroie and St Pierre. The mix of the fish depends on the textures. The rouille here is bright yellow, from saffron, and spicy from chilli. Diners are given raw, unpeeled cloves of garlic to rub on their croûtons. Other rouilles can be a garlic purée mixed with oil and chilli; or roasted sweet peppers, breadcrumbs and oil according to others. Elizabeth David attributes sophisticated variations to the Voile d'Or in St-Raphaël: grilled and skinned peppers, pounded with lobster coral and sea urchins; or a cooked seaweed sweetened with pastis.

This restaurant version is from the Brasserie des Catalans in Marseilles, and is served with rouille, aïoli, and a chilled bottle of Provence rosé. Soup and fish are two separate courses. The unusual boiling is necessary to break down the lesser fish and form a sound base.

BOUILLABAISSE

THE SOUP: Soften 2 onions, 2 leeks, 4 cloves of garlic, 2 tomatoes, parsley, dried fennel, shallot, and a red pepper in oil. Add the firm fish – rascasse, weever, John Dory, conger, gurnard – 4 sliced potatoes and hot water. Boil strongly for about 15 minutes, depending on the size of the fish. Season with black pepper. Add crawfish. Cook for 5 minutes, then add prawns and any soft fish like wrasse. Cook on for 10 minutes. Season with saffron.

THE ROUILLE: Crush 2 small red peppers with garlic. Soak bread in fish stock, and mash to a paste with the peppers and garlic. Add a fine line of oil, and dilute with fish stock.

TO SERVE: Remove potatoes, prawns, crawfish. Strain the soup. Serve with fried bread rubbed with garlic, the rouille, an aïoli and the fish to the side.

Further north, the boats take the identical catch up the Rhône. Point followed the same idea, but adapted it to inland, restaurant use. He marinated his fish in oil and tomato purée, with fennel, anise and saffron for twelve hours, then cooked the fish in the marinade. To these, he would add a bouillabaisse base made separately and thickened with cream and egg yolks, and serve hot with an aïoli.

THE BÉARNAISE

The other side of the hollandaise family is more refined, and has been husbanded carefully through the classical kitchen. The béarnaise is younger than a hollandaise, but more extended and perfumed. It is credited to a chef working for Henri IV, the first monarch to recognize the guild of chefs, so it deserves a special place as a more courtly variation of a hollandaise.

The technique is the same, except the base of water and vinegar is infused with diced, poached shallots (or spring onions), French tarragon, chervil and peppercorns. These gutsy scents give it enough allure to stand up to the stronger fish which usually go for grilling: salmon, mackerel and, more recently, tuna. Swap the tarragon for mint, and the sauce is Paloise and vigorous enough to accompany young lamb in early summer. Add tomato paste, and it becomes a Choron for poached eggs or grilled veal chops. Whip in a little melted meat glaze or demi-glace, and it becomes a Valois and can live with a tournedos or sweetbreads.

Out of this side of the family come a series of well-flavoured sauces, designed mostly to stand up to stronger meats and cooking methods, and each in turn with the seasoning raised a notch.

Tyrolienne is an extraordinary hybrid, a bastardization of hollandaise and mayonnaise.

TYROLIENNE: Reduce the herbs, shallots and vinegar as for a béarnaise; season the egg yolks with tomato purée; build the sauce up with oil. Serve with grilled foods.

Gribiche uses hard-boiled eggs, a useful trick in the salmonella era.

GRIBICHE: Mix the yolks of 6 hard-boiled eggs with a teaspoon of mustard; build the sauce up with oil. Finish with chopped egg whites, capers, gherkins, diced parsley, tarragon and chervil.

Tartar has almost fallen out of use, except as commercial sachets and packets, but is a pedigree sauce. The technique is identical to a gribiche, but the finish is with a purée of spring onions and/or chervil.

BEURRE BLANC

The *beurre blanc* is a sauce of supreme technique and subtlety, the emblem of modern cooking. Like the rouille, it has no eggs. Without them, there is little help in stabilizing the sauce beyond sleight of hand.

In one of those rather-too-neat stories that speckle the history of cooking, the *beurre blanc* is credited to a cook in Nantes who forgot her eggs for a béarnaise one evening and improvised. It was, so the story has it, such a success she went on to open a restaurant on the strength of it. Either way, this was the sauce of the concierges of Paris, the mothers of Lyons, and of numerous restaurants along the banks of the Loire where it was used to sauce dry fish, like pike and shad. At its most simple, it is not much more than a glass of wine mixed with butter.

BEURRE BLANC

STAGE 1: Dice the shallots, sweat in wine, properly a dry Loire wine like Muscadet or Vouvray. Add salt, if the butter to be used is unsalted. Herbs are an option. Reduce this liquid to a scant tablespoon. If too strong, it can be diluted later with water. The base taste will be of the wine. At this juncture, some recipes include a little fish stock and reduce further, or a little cream to help stabilize. The liquor can be strained and wrung out of a cloth to clean the last precious, acidic droplets, or left as it is with the softened shallots and herbs adding texture and colour.

STAGE 2: Take the pan off the heat to cool. Dice the butter into small cubes, not bigger than the top of a little finger. Like the wine, the butter should not have picked up any other flavours in the fridge, be fresh and of good quality, and probably lactic (Norman or Dutch). The water in it creates the emulsification. As with a hollandaise, add a piece at a time. Whisk vigorously and rhythmically, crossing the pan over the flame to speed up or slow down the process as each piece incorporates. The agitation of the whisk causes the amalgamation, not the heat. A thick, warm (not hot), opaque, cream white sauce is the result. Season with lemon. Correctly done, the butter becomes a vehicle for other flavours: roasted garlic, rosemary, ginger, orange, lemon, lime; some of the wine sometimes substituted with vinegars to increase the acidity.

In a sense, there is no one *beurre blanc*. Each one changes according to the butter, the wine, the juices. It is a technique, rather than a dish. Even Marguery's sole has an echo of the same methodology. The overriding virtue is that the *beurre blanc* is cooked to order, uses the juices to hand, and concentrates them quickly. It takes on the stature of some of the classical sauces: humbler, meeker, but just as charming, perhaps more so. Carême's whole days of stocks to achieve his aspics, are telescoped into ten or twenty minutes of activity.

FISH STOCKS

The *beurre blanc* also seems to be much more a part of fish cooking. This is the fragile side of the craft; not the assertive, fractious bullying of meat cookery. It is the slow assertion of heat, the gentle tightening of the tourniquet, a long curve, not a steep cliff. Every aspect is more delicate. The process is micro-technology: either hurried along so it can be carried out under the total gaze of the chef, or else stretched out and slowed right down so the crucial points in the equation are drawn out and the risks minimized.

Even in stock cooking, the bones and heads should be only simmered. James Lascelles wrote a whole book, *The Advanced Fish Cook*, dedicated to persuading the English to stop boiling their fish. Breaths of movement on the surface of the water are what are needed, not belches and bubbles.

Sole and turbot were the prime bones for the classical fish stock, partly because they were available, and also because they give a good result. The modern kitchen has been content to make a stock from the bones and trimmings of whatever white fish it is cooking. Some restaurants make two stocks, one for cooking and one for sauces.

A classical kitchen added the aromatics at the end of the process, because the liquid would have been flavoured and reduced later. It was a catch-all that had different applications, probably wrapped inside one of the mother sauces, certainly thickened with flour and butter, so it had no need to be distinct. The modern kitchen uses its stocks at the last minute, and needs a more definite article. Escoffier defined these as essences, rather than stocks. He used the trimmings of mushrooms, onions, parsley stalks and the juice of a lemon.

A CLASSICAL FISH STOCK

Soak the bones. Add to cold water. Bring to a simmer. Add diced vegetables and herbs. Simmer 20 minutes. Strain.

A MODERN FISH STOCK OR A CLASSICAL FISH ESSENCE

Soak the bones. Sweat diced vegetables. Add the bones. Sweat on. Deglaze with a little wine. Cover with water. Bring to a simmer and skim. Add herbs. Simmer 20 minutes.

HERBS AND AROMATICS

The modern kitchen has brought many more tastes into play. Perm from different groups: onion, carrot, leek, celery, courgette, garlic; cinnamon, clove, star anise, peppercorn, allspice; bay, thyme, parsley, fennel, tarragon, marjoram, basil, chervil, coriander, juniper; lemon, orange, lime.

This choice of aromatics led the kitchen to seek out more alliances with vegetables and herbs. The classical kitchen had not necessarily used stocks to cook fish, and had been content to make up lighter vinegar- or wine-based courtbouillons. Lighter stocks had attractive uses. Something as direct as an infusion of rosemary, thyme, marjoram and basil could be as good, perhaps even better, than a poaching stock. Down this road, the stock could be used to start a *beurre blanc* that was already imbued with the fish's own taste. The whole vat-stock system was short-circuited.

Vegetable stocks had other uses, not least if made with good wines and generous amounts of garlic, as a cure for over-reduced meat sauces. They are short processes:

MODERN VEGETABLE STOCK: 1

Dice vegetables. Cover with boiling water. Cook for 5 minutes. Add herbs and seasoning. Take off the heat. Infuse 10 minutes. Strain.

MODERN VEGETABLE STOCK: 2

Soften an onion in a casserole. Add diced vegetables and fruits to season. Sweat. Add a base of washed, soaked lentils. Cover with water. Bring to a simmer. Skim. Cook for an hour. Skim off any froth. Strain.

The ushering of vegetables up the scale, was a signpost for the way ahead.

KING SALMON: FIRST APPROACHES

THE BRITISH SUMMER meal of the first fish, simmered *à l'anglaise*; the first digging of new potatoes with early shoots of mint; a salad of cucumbers; strawberries, was one of the bench marks of the culinary year.

Salmon are at their peak. They make their run in from the ocean, back to the river where they were born. Fit, well-fed, the sea lice still on their scales, they come inland to spawn. Out of salted waters, they will not feed.

WHEN THE FLESH SEIZES

In areas where salmon are fished, recipes are streamlined and unaffected. The poaching liquid does not need to be grand. A few strong, deliberate flavours suffice. A seventeenth century English recipe suggests making a liquor of beer, salt, parsley, thyme, rosemary and a good measure of sharp vinegar.

In Wales, milk often replaced the courtbouillon completely, perhaps seasoned with fennel which could be chopped to make a sauce thickened with flour; or else the sauce might have been neat cream. Old cookery books say salmon should be boiled for ten minutes to the pound; baked for twenty-five for the first two-and-a-half pounds and then ten minutes for each pound over. The modern kitchen has taken these times right back, seeking the optimum point between cooked and uncooked; when the flesh seizes, and changes its allegiance from vertical to horizontal. If the cooking time is less than half-an-hour, then the courtbouillon should be made up ahead. The technique is about simplicity and confidence.

SALMON À L'ANGLAISE

Place the whole fish in a kettle, with enough water or herbed courtbouillon to cover. Bring to a simmer. Take off the heat. Leave to stand in the liquid, 20 minutes to serve hot, 4 hours to serve cold.

The same tortoise-sure pace applies to dry cooking: the fish lain out on foil, herbs stuffed inside the belly, wetted with wine, the foil sealed up into a parcel and placed in the lowest of ovens. Cook one hour, maybe two. Slow and low is the optimum. Farmed fish, being fattier, need a longer cooking time than wild, perhaps ten per cent more.

STRONG FLAVOURS

The size of the salmon made it a regular and impressive feature of the classical table. Escoffier insisted it should be served with two sauces. 'Most suitable are anchovy, caper, shrimp, Genèvoise, hollandaise, lobster, oyster, mousseline, nantua (béchamel with cream and crayfish butter), nut, ravigote (cold, a vinaigrette; hot, a herb velouté), and Venitienne (white wine and tarragon).'

The complex and elongated Genèvoise pre-dates Escoffier, and is chronicled by Carême.

SAUCE GENÈVOISE AFTER CARÊME

Sweat onions, carrots, parsley in butter. Add the salmon head. Cover. Stew 15 minutes. Drain off the butter. Add 1¾ pints red wine. Reduce by half. Add 18 fl oz fish espagnol. Simmer 1 hour. Strain. Rest. Strain. Add 18 fl oz red wine, and the same amount of fish stock. Simmer. Skim. Reduce. Strain. Finish with a tablespoon of anchovy essence, and 5oz butter.

FLAVOURS PAIRED

There are many examples in regional cooking of the salmon being paired with tough, muscular flavours. Families along the Teifi served a dish of salmon steaks baked with butter, port, ketchup and boned anchovy.

An old dish from the Wye river valley flakes the salmon after it has been poached, blends it with breadcrumbs, flaked eel, mushrooms, butter, eggs, clove and nutmeg, wetted with wine and lemon. The farce was spread out on a thickness of pastry; the steaks laid out on top;

garnished with oysters; the pastry sealed and baked for forty-five minutes. A Shropshire pie was baked with shrimps.

In Northumberland, a poaching liquor of vinegar, white wine, pepper, mace and cloves was used to marinate and preserve steaks, which were then re-heated and served on toast. More often the acid, tart fruits come into play – gooseberries, strawberries, redcurrants, tomatoes, passion fruit, apples – often allied to something from the dairy. To the modern kitchen, these were the flavours for cutting a thick hollandaise or seasoning an aromatic *beurre blanc*, deposing the more direct acidity of lemon.

OLD IDEAS REVIVED

This is an even more fundamental version from Franco Taruschio at the Walnut Tree Inn at Llandewi Skirrid, just outside Abergavenny. The dish is symptomatic of the restaurant itself – part roadside trattoria, part brasserie, part pub with wine – expedient and pragmatic, easily cooked and yet having the graces of something much more sophisticated. Taruschio, although well-versed in classical technique, qualifies as an increasingly respected modern chef. Since the early Sixties he has fostered and developed new supplies for his restaurant in an area which never had such a tradition and which now, via Vin Sullivan, supplies many restaurants in the west country with speciality produce. This produce forms the core of his menu.

SALMON WITH RHUBARB AFTER
FRANCO TARUSCHIO

Chop a stick of rhubarb. Half-cover with water. Add a knob of butter. Cook 5 minutes. Take out half the rhubarb. Reduce the rest. Cream. In a separate, non-stick pan, fry the salmon steaks for 1 minute either side. Plate the steaks. Pour over the sauce, and garnish with the reserved rhubarb.

Ginger is another colourful flavouring that goes right back into English cooking. In the *Good Huswife's Jewel*, dated 1696, Thomas Dawson recommends putting the salmon in pastry with currants and ginger. Two of the most elegant post-war English restaurant cooks have made a feature of this dish. One is Francis Coulson at Sharrow Bay on Ullswater, the first of the country house hotels; the other is George Perry-Smith, at the subterranean Hole in the Wall at Bath, and later at the Riverside, Helford.

Perry-Smith's repertoire otherwise concentrated on the Elizabeth David territory of more southerly French bourgeois cooking. This is his final restaurant version of the salmon, arrived at around 1986, after many years of variations, considerably more buttery and gingery than the version given earlier in Jane Grigson's *Fish Cookery*. '*T*o *the disappointment of those who would like everything just so, days, tastes, ginger and especially the salmon itself, all vary. I would not make it with farmed salmon, as a general rule, whereas farmed salmon is pretty good for smoking; and I would like to know which way the salmon was going, and when. So you have to make some judgements of your own.*

'*Have an all-butter pastry ready. Prepare a ginger and currant butter, by chopping 6–7 globes of preserved ginger and mixing them with 2oz currants, salt and pepper and a 250g packet of butter. This should be enough for seven 8–9oz parcels of salmon, each for two people, and 6oz pastry should be enough to wrap each parcel. Skin and bone the salmon, reassemble it into 8–9oz portions made up of two equal layers, season well, spread each layer with ginger butter. Roll out the pastry as thinly as you comfortably can, but don't risk any holes, and keep the turnings to a minimum; the packets must be thoroughly sealed. Place each parcel on a square of buttered foil, and bake in a hot oven for 27 minutes. Serve with plenty of sauce messine.*'

The sauce is from Lorraine, and another distant relative of the hollandaise family.

SAUCE MESSINE

Chop half-a-dozen sprigs of tarragon, parsley and chervil with 2 small shallots. Work together 2oz butter with a teaspoon of flour, 1 of French mustard, beaten yolks of 2 eggs and ½ pint single cream. Blend in the herbs, and heat in a bain-marie, stirring all the time. Do not boil. Season with lemon.

Francis Coulson enjoys telling the story of the taxi driver who first dropped him off at the isolated cottages in 1949 with his pots and pans and called out after him: 'I'll pick you up next week.' His version of the dish adds four ounces of diced cucumber, to two each of ginger and currants.

His pastry is puff, where Grigson's is short crust made with eight ounces of flour to five of butter and a single egg. Coulson's sauce, like his cooking, leans more to the classic hotel school than the regional.

Sweat 3 diced shallots in ½oz butter and the trimmings from the stem ginger. Add ½ pint fish stock and ½ pint white wine, and reduce to a syrup. Add 1 pint double cream and reduce. Add the juice of ½ lemon, and beat in 1oz butter. Season and strain.

SOUTHERN INFLUENCES

Other big fish in other parts of Europe have been treated with similar force. Escoffier gives a recipe for large fish, allowed to cook in a court-bouillon, let go cold, and sauced with equal amounts of grated horse-radish, skinned chopped walnuts, sugar, salt, lemon juice and enough cream to create a sauce the texture of an emulsification. But the modern kitchen has given up on such long cooking, even with pastry which was, in any event, often used originally as a form of packaging akin to tin foil, and not necessarily eaten. The parcel inflates under a grill, and can be broken open at the table to release an aromatic volcano.

SALMON WITH HERBS AND WINE

Lay the salmon fillet on foil. Add herbs, butter, a tablespoon of wine or stronger alcohol like Campari. Seal. Bake or grill.

Salmon benefits from precise cooking more than other fish. Like beef or lamb, it can go through stages of cooking: rare, medium and well done. While it was hidden away under one of Escoffier's two sauces, this was an unappreciated subtlety. The idea was imported from cultures on either side of the Pacific, used to more anaemic southerly fish.

The Japanese sushi chef cuts thumb-sized raw slices out of the belly of the fish, and serves them naked bar a pile of the powerful green root-horseradish, *wasabi*. In Latin and South America, meanwhile, wafer thin raw fillets are cured with just a squeeze of lemon, lime or orange for a few minutes, to make ceviches.

DIRECT ATTACKS

If these cooks could serve fish raw, or nearly so, why bundle it up in layers of heat like some perspiring baby in swaddling clothes? To the classical cook the salmon might have represented a starting point for his ideas, but for the modern chef, anxious to represent faithfully the taste of the fish itself, there was no reason to go down that avenue. There were more abbreviated, direct attacks, and one at least from closer to home: gravlax. In place of citrus, salt drew out the natural juices and mixed them with seasonings like dill and aquavit.

Anna's Place, in Stoke Newington, has evolved from brasserie to studied restaurant and back to a Scandinavian bistro, but the gravlax has survived the different incarnations. The gracious and charming Anna Hegarty uses a deep wooden trough shaped like a canoe to take the length of the fish. One fillet is lain across the other.

GRAVLAX AFTER ANNA HEGARTY

Wipe a 1½lb middle cut of salmon dry. Divide in 2 along the backbone and carefully remove all the bones – you can feel them if you stroke the surface with your fingertips, and they can be easily pulled out with pliers or tweezers.

Mix 6 tablespoons sugar, 3 of salt and ½ of crushed white peppercorns, and rub this well into both sides of the salmon. Sandwich the pieces of salmon together with dill, laying the fleshy sides together and the thin part against the thick.

Lay the salmon in a dish high enough to hold it, sprinkle with a good handful of dill and a little of the reserved spices. Turn it skin-side down, top with more mixed spices and dill. Place a chopping board or something similar on top, and a weight of some kind (a couple of cartons of orange juice will do). This will keep the salmon under pressure.

Chill the salmon for at least 24–36 hours, preferably a couple of days. Turn now and then during this time. Then scrape off the seasoning, and discard the liquid which has accumulated in the dish.

Cut the salmon off the skin, in angled slices, about 1 inch thick. The skin is cut in ¼-inch strips which are fried, skin-side down, in a very hot pan until almost burned. Serve as an accompaniment to the dill-cured fish.

The usual accompaniment is a hot sorrel sauce or creamed spinach, but in early spring the first shoots of nettles provide a more traditional touch.

FISH SAUCE WITH NETTLES AFTER
ANNA HEGARTY

Reduce by half, 2 cups of good fish stock made from the bones and trimmings of white fish, and 1½ cups white wine. Whisk in 2½oz butter. Season a cup of *crème fraîche* with anise, fennel and salt, and add to the stock.

Blanch 2oz of the first nettles, about ½ inch long, chop and add to the sauce.

This is a more conventional dill sauce to go with the cold gravlax.

THE DRESSING: To 1 part mustard, 1 part vinegar, 1 part sugar and 6 parts sunflower oil dribbled, as for mayonnaise, into 3 parts soured cream, add 1 cup chopped dill.

The technique for gravlax is uncannily similar to smoking salmon. For smoking, salmon are salted for twelve hours, rinsed off, and only then placed on racks to be cold smoked for another twelve to eighteen hours. The smoke in Scotland is usually oak, or hardwoods like beech and chestnut. In America, hickory is preferred. In Canada, maple.

A MODERN DISH

The classical kitchen revered smoked salmon, and for lesser restaurants it provided the perfect compromise between the cautious customer and the waiter who mistrusted his kitchen, or whose kitchen was not all it seemed.

Raymond Blanc devised a tartar for his move from his original small shoe-box of a restaurant in the modern suburb of Oxford Summertown, to the old English yellow-stone manor in the thatched village of Great Milton, Le Manoir aux Quat'Saisons. It is a dish that has been widely taken up in other restaurants, who have altered the fish and the seasonings. There are elements of both ceviche and gravlax and, in one of those charming touches that characterize much of Blanc's work, there is the polite use of the Englishness of cucumber. A one-pound weight of fillet will stretch to perhaps ten portions.

TARTAR OF SALMON AFTER RAYMOND BLANC

THE SALMON: Lay a skinned fillet of salmon on cling film, and smear with salt, lemon and dill on both sides. Seal, and leave for 12 hours. Rinse off the cure and dice the salmon into ⅛th-inch cubes. Mix ½ teaspoon mustard, 2 teaspoons soured cream, lemon and pepper and bind the salmon.

THE SALAD: Peel a cucumber. Cut in half lengthways, scoop out the seeds, slice very finely. Sprinkle with salt, leave to macerate 30 minutes, rinse off. Pat dry and dress lightly with a mix of 1 part wine vinegar to 2 parts non-scented oil. Prepare the garnish of finely cut triangular sections of lemon and chopped fresh dill.

TO SERVE: Using a pastry cutter per portion as a mould, fill 9/10ths full with the salmon, top with soured cream, decorate with a circle of dill and wedges of lemon and a mound of caviar in the centre. Surround the base with overlapping circles of cucumber. Serve with warm toast.

The idea of salmon tartar is not unique. Variations are found in the Loire, but these are much more rustic, unrefined and have their parentage more obviously with French cooking and the hollandaise family.

TARTAR OF SALMON FROM THE LOIRE

Dice a fillet of raw salmon. Mix with egg yolks. Season with capers. Dribble in olive oil as if making a mayonnaise to bind.

HOT SMOKED SALMON

Dishes of hot smoked salmon are rare. Smoke is an unwieldy, delinquent, all-dominating flavour that needs a tight rein. One means of control is for the kitchen to do the smoking itself.

In Chinese cooking the smoking is sometimes done in a wok, but in this dish Jurg Munch at the Mandarin Hotel in Hong Kong cold smokes the fillet for just five minutes to give the merest hint of taste without letting the smoke dominate.

SALMON WITH VEGETABLE VINAIGRETTE

THE SAUCE: Cut into cubes 20g carrot, courgette, cooked artichoke bottom and celery; 10g red peppers, kiwi and cucumber; 5g truffles. Combine with 60ml red wine vinegar, 120ml virgin olive oil and 30ml walnut oil.

THE SALMON: Lightly smoke for 5 minutes. Lay a 160g fillet per person on buttered greaseproof paper. Season with butter and salt. Bake at not more than 80–100°C for 15–20 minutes. The low heat allows the salmon to retain its natural juices without overcooking or changing colour.

HORSERADISH CREAM: Combine 80g whipped cream with 40g freshly grated horseradish and a dash of vinegar. Season with salt and pepper.

TO SERVE: Lay the salmon on the sauce, with a tablespoon of cream to the side.

The smoke can be used as a seasoning, or even as a protection. John

Radford developed this idea while head chef at Handsells in Edinburgh, one of those shooting stars in British catering which had closed by the time it was getting recognition.

TWO KINDS OF SALMON WITH A CRAYFISH SAUCE AFTER JOHN RADFORD

THE SAUCE: Dice shallots. Simmer in white wine and vinegar coloured with saffron. Reduce by half. Add crayfish tails or crayfish stock, and reduce further. Mount with butter as in a hollandaise.

THE SALMON: Smear a fillet of salmon with the sauce. Lay a thin slice of smoked salmon on top. Glaze with more sauce. Grill swiftly.

TO SERVE: Lay the salmon on bed of crisp vegetables, surround with the sauce and garnish with the crayfish tails.

THE USE OF SOUR TASTES

The *beurre blanc* owes its parentage to the signature dish of the whole *nouvelle cuisine* era: salmon with sorrel. The Troisgros brothers at Roanne made this dish their own: the richness of the fish blunting the acidity of the sorrel, and the creaminess of the butter.

In restaurant mythology the station, right by their restaurant, is said to have been painted pink and green after the dish. Over the years they have given different variations of the recipe, sometimes with cream and sometimes without. The initial reduction shows the marriage of the classical, organized male kitchen with the female technique. No longer do we just start with a glass of wine and a shallot. The sauce can be made ahead so that the salmon does not have to sit around waiting, as it did in the classical kitchen.

SALMON WITH SORREL AFTER THE TROISGROS BROTHERS

THE SAUCE: Reduce a glass of white wine, 450ml fish stock, ¼ glass vermouth, 2 chopped shallots and ½ teaspoon of demi-glace. Cream. Add 30g chopped sorrel. Take off the heat. Whip in 100g butter. Season with salt, pepper and lemon.

THE SALMON: Wipe both sides of the fillets with oil. Sauté briefly in hot oil. Serve the fish on the sauce.

Other greening agents like spinach or watercress produce a deeper green colour, but lack the acidity. But with a herb like basil the whole technique can be stood on its head and the acidity brought into play at the very end, as with a classical hollandaise.

SALMON WITH BASIL

THE SAUCE: Sweat shallots in butter. Add basil. Deglaze with Noilly. Add fish stock. Reduce. Cream. Mount with butter as for hollandaise. Finish with lemon.

THE SALMON: Fry the salmon fillets without oil or butter in a non-stick pan. Finish with a single squeeze of lemon. Serve on the sauce.

The souring of sauces with lemon, sorrel or vinegar has become a crucial element in modern cooking, as much a feature as sugar in Cantonese cooking, or flour to the classical cook. Not a wall of taste, as in an over-vinegared vinaigrette, but just a note using milder wine vinegars, to pick out the other flavours.

SKATE: A FISH APART

SKATE LIVERS WERE once prized, but these rarely now get to market. Unlike other fish, the gelatinous, fibrous flesh benefits from a day or two's keeping. The *Guide Culinaire* lists only three recipes: a gratin; deep fried; and, its most universal application, with black butter, a rural technique, swift, one-dimensional and striking, yet peripheral to most of the classical repertoire, appearing only occasionally to sauce eggs or brains.

SKATE WITH BLACK BUTTER

THE BUTTER: Heat some good butter in a pan until it begins to sizzle and turn brown. Take off the heat. Strain. Add a few drops of vinegar.

THE FISH: Cut the wings into fillets. Poach in a courtbouillon with vinegar. Remove the fish, and place in the oven to dry for a minute. Wet a clean pan with a tablespoon of stock, add lemon or vinegar, parsley and capers. Add the fish briefly, then finish in the pan with half the butter. Plate, pour the sauce over the fish and top with the last of the butter.

The flesh is resilient and adapts comfortably to the tougher styles of cooking like roasting or braising. Escoffier held that braising was the most difficult of all techniques. 'Only by long experience and by careful attention to detail can a cook expect to become familiar with its problems.' It is perhaps easier in modern ovens, with their consistent temperature controls.

BRAISED SKATE WITH CIDER AFTER PAUL GAYLER

THE FISH: Sweat a base of diced shallot, tomato and apple in a heat-proof dish. Add the skate in steaks, a glass of cider and 1 of fish stock. Cook in a low oven for 10–15 minutes. Take out, and set the fish aside.

THE SAUCE: Strain the sauce. Reduce. Cream. Finish with butter, and correct the seasoning using more cider or calvados.

This next variation is interesting because at the very last it goes back to the classical idea of a parsley butter to finish the sauce.

BRAISED SKATE WITH ONIONS AFTER JACQUES MAXIMIN

THE ONIONS: Peel some small onions. Put in a pan with enough water to come half way up them. Add a knob of butter. Cook for about 40 minutes.

THE FISH: Add the skate as steaks, and a glass of wine. Continue to cook slowly for 15 minutes. Remove fish and onions.

THE SAUCE: Reduce the sauce by half. Finish by whisking in parsley butter.

As in the black butter dish, skate lends itself to standing for a few minutes after poaching, while the sauce is being made up. Unlike most other fish, it might even be an advantage. The long grooves of the flesh harbour droplets of the poaching liquid which can water down any sauce.

SKATE SALAD AFTER JOHN BURTON-RACE

THE FISH: Cut the steaks and place in a steamer. Add a minimum of water, lemon butter and soy. Steam quickly. Remove the fish.

THE SAUCE: Bind the juices with a fruity olive oil spiked with shallot and chives.

TO SERVE: Shred the skate and lay on a bed of mixed lettuces and a diced tomato. Pour the sauce round.

This is a more rustic version.

SKATE SALAD AFTER ALISON DAVY

THE FISH: Poach the skate in a courtbouillon. Remove, and set aside.

THE SALAD: Heat oil in a pan. Add garlic. Fry some croûtons. In a second pan, fry some bacon in strips until crisp. Arrange a green salad of different leaves. Toss on the croûtons and the bacon.

TO SERVE: Shred the skate. Warm through in the bacon fat. Lay on top of the salad.

Given its ability to cross over into the province of meat cookery, skate has potential for experiment. Just as it can cope with flavours like bacon, so it can also combine well with other fish. Filleted, it can be rolled up around a stuffing or else, as in this startling recipe from John Kenward of Kenwards in Lewes, it plays off with fish, fruit and vegetable. Kenward prefers to bake, rather than poach, his fish, and to cook it on the bone.

SKATE WITH SQUID, LEEKS AND ORANGE
AFTER JOHN KENWARD

THE SQUID: Take off the head and tentacles. Put in cold water with onions, garlic and other vegetables to make a stock. Poach for about 10 minutes. Take out the squid, remove its eyes and beak and put those back into the stock. Clean the squid and slice into finger lengths. The stock can be held back as the basis for other fish sauces. The ink sac will turn it black for a colourful effect, or can be used as a colourant on its own.

THE SKATE: Cut an insert into the backbone of the skate, and stuff with spring onion and garlic. Bake in a medium oven. Take out and shred.

THE SAUCE: Slice leeks diagonally and poach briefly. In a second pan, stir-fry the shredded skate, the squid lengths, leeks and shredded sections of orange. Deglaze with a little fish stock.

RED MULLET: CHANGING FASHIONS

THE GREEKS AND Romans prized red mullet so highly that it became one of the most expensive fish in the ancient world. The French word *rouget* applies to the whole *mullidae* family. Escoffier said the best were the red rock fish, from the Mediterranean. But they are also found off the western European coast as far south as the Canary Islands, and as far north as Norway in summer.

Large numbers came into English west coast ports in the last century, and it was fashionable to go to the south-west ports just to eat red mullet. An old Weymouth recipe suggests rolling them in flour, wrapping in paper along with grated onion, parsley, fennel, mushrooms and a little sherry, and baking for half-an-hour.

This sort of rough treatment does not seem in keeping with the delicate, distinctive flesh that so sets mullet out from both the family of white fish and also the larger, oilier fish, though it works well for lesser fish, like farmed trout. The bullet-shaped head, in some species as blunt as the engine of an InterCity 125 express; the silver flesh and red skin, give it the clothes of an alien interloper, from another ocean. It has no gall bladder, which is what makes the livers of other fish bitter. The French nicknamed it the woodcock of the seas, since the woodcock is generally cooked undrawn. The liver is in itself a delicacy. Frédy Girardet, who has turned the *hôtel de ville* in the small town of Crissier outside Lausanne into one of the great modern restaurants, creates a haunting *beurre blanc* with them.

RED MULLET WITH ROSEMARY
AFTER FRÉDY GIRARDET

THE FUMET: Fillet the mullet. Reserve the livers. Make a fumet with head and bones by sweating in butter, adding diced shallot and a good sprig of rosemary, mix well and then add a glass of white wine and 1 of water. Cook 5 minutes. Sieve.

THE SAUCE: Reduce the fumet by half. Add cream and reduce to thicken. Whisk in the butter, a piece at a time. Add the chopped livers. Season with salt, pepper and lemon.

THE FISH: Fry the fillets briefly on each side in butter, in a non-stick pan. Serve on the sauce and garnish with rosemary.

Other flavours apart from rosemary combine well: cumin, orange, a little garlic, the whole family of Provençal ground level seasonings suit. The butter sauce is an arrogant gesture of how modern kitchens stride from one market to the next and can even mix a fish usually associated with the southern, oil-based cultures, with the butter of the north. This recipe, also from Girardet, stays closer to the flavourings more usually found.

RED MULLET WITH HERBS AND TOMATO

THE FISH: Fillet the mullet. Warm a little oil in a pan. Sweat a diced shallot. Lay on the fillets. Cook 2 minutes either side. Remove and keep warm.

THE SAUCE: Dice 1 tablespoonful each fresh herbs, garlic and tomato per person. Add to the pan. Deglaze with wine. Pour over the fillets.

Filleting the fish is an affectation of the modern restaurant in deference to customers' concern over the bones. But in both classical and regional cookery, mullet was mostly char-grilled whole. It was a fish of the barbecue. The smoke prints itself on the charred skin. Escoffier gives recipes for marinades of lemon, oil, salt, pepper and fennel before grilling. The sides are slashed to let the oil seep in. For bigger fish, not often seen these days, he includes recipes for meat stuffings, with the fish filleted and re-formed with the stuffing down the bone tract. Simpler and more direct, Elizabeth David gives a recipe for a mullet char-grilled with a branch of fennel in its stomach, and brought to the table alight with Armagnac.

The modern kitchen, though, has tended to look for a more sophisticated visual result. Chris Oakes who, from being head chef at the Castle at Taunton moved to his own restaurant in an old girls' school on the outskirts of Stroud, makes up for the lack of bones in the cooking process, by braising like meat.

FILLET OF RED MULLET BAKED WITH BRAISED ONIONS, TOMATO AND THYME AND SERVED ON A ROSTI POTATO WITH A CREAM SAUCE

THE ONIONS: Peel and slice 1 large onion per person. Cover the bottom of a thick-bottomed pan with oil. Add the onions and stir. Lower the heat, cover, and stew for 5–10 minutes until they start to caramelize. Add a little cold water and stir. Repeat until the onions are soft and most of the liquid has evaporated. Season with salt and pepper and set aside.

THE TOMATO: Blanch, refresh and peel ½ tomato per person. Scoop out the seeds and dice the flesh neatly. Pick off the leaves of a sprig of thyme and add. Set aside.

THE SAUCE: Reduce ½ pint fish stock by three-quarters. Add 3 fl oz white wine, and reduce again by three-quarters. Take off the heat and whisk in 2oz butter to emulsify. Season, and keep warm. (This is enough for four. The stock could be replaced by 4 fl oz vermouth, in which case add another 2oz butter to mellow the sauce.)

THE ROSTI: Peel and grate ½ a large new potato per person on a cheese grater. Dry in a clean towel. Cover the bottom of a small, thick pan with oil and add enough potato for one serving. Fry on both sides until golden brown.

THE FISH: Scale and fillet the mullet, leaving the skin on. Lay the fish on the braised onions in a braising dish. Scatter the tomato mix on top. Season. Wet the bottom of the pan with enough wine just to cover all the surface. Cover with kitchen foil. Cook for 10–12 minutes at gas 7, 425°F (220°C). Take out and keep warm.

TO SERVE: Place the warmed potato in the centre of a warmed plate. Lay the fish and onions on the potato and surround with the sauce. Serve immediately.

The colours also lend themselves to a salad, as in this dish from Alan Holland at the stately Mallory Court in Leamington Spa.

RED MULLET VINAIGRETTE AFTER
ALAN HOLLAND

THE VINAIGRETTE: Peel, seed and chop a tomato. Finely chop a bunch of basil leaves. Add to 275ml extra virgin olive oil, along with ¼ clove crushed garlic, ½ a finely chopped shallot, 1 teaspoon sherry vinegar, 2 bay leaves, salt and pepper. Macerate for 4–5 days.

THE FISH: Fillet the mullet. Steam over fish stock for about 3 minutes and allow to rest for 5 minutes. Remove the bay leaves from the dressing, and spoon the oil on to a warm plate. Arrange the fillets on top. Garnish with olives, shredded basil and cherry tomatoes.

Red mullet has one weakness. The flesh suffers in poaching. Rick Stein of the Seafood Restaurant at Padstow has devised an ingenious trick using seaweed as a bed to lift the fish out of the water so it steams instead; a sort of aquatic barbecue. Bladderwrack is the most commonly found seaweed on British beaches, and imprints a very definite taste of the sea on the dish.

RED MULLET WITH SEAWEED AFTER RICK STEIN

THE SEAWEED: Blanch the seaweed in a large pan for 1 minute. Wash well. Place the seaweed in a pan just large enough to fit the fish across. Cover the seaweed with fish stock, bring to a simmer and then turn right down.

THE FISH: Lay the unfilleted fish on the seaweed, cover, and cook gently for up to 10 minutes. Take out the fish and keep warm.

THE SAUCE: Strain off the stock. Reduce rapidly by two-thirds. Finish with butter.

THE SCALLOP: A CHAMELEON

THE MODEST SCALLOP, with its plain white, grooved shell, religious inheritance and underwater agility, was one of the first fish to be ushered back into the new vocabulary. Once the symbol of the pilgrims on the road to the shrine of St James at Compostela, the scallop found a new role as a purveyor of other flavours, a culinary chameleon that can take on the hues of different seasonings without losing its own identity.

Escoffier had called for scallops to be poached for six to seven minutes, even before embarking on a recipe. But these must have been long-bearded, large beasts that had sat on the ocean floor for a good many years. The modern kitchen cut the cooking times back, sometimes to less than a minute, to retain their sweetness, and deals exclusively with the younger fish or the thumb-nail queenies.

Strangely, both regional and classical cooking are littered with examples of vigorous flavourings that seem now to take little account of the fish's sensitivity. Early recipes take a perverse delight in using the acidic and the citrus. André Simon credits, 'Elizabeth, commonly called Joan Cromwell, wife of the later Usurper', with seasoning scallops with ginger, nutmeg, cinnamon and sugar, and mashing them up with wine vinegar and breadcrumbs; and, worse still, mixing them with oyster liquor and gravy, dissolved anchovies, minced onions, thyme and the juice of a lemon.

Hannah Glasse, writing in 1747, recommends mace and orange with a béchamel style sauce. Scottish recipes rolled the poor things in oatmeal before frying, while in East Anglia they were marinated in lemon and then rolled up with ham, breadcrumbs, Cheddar and onion before deep frying.

Such dressings in winter clothes suggest either a deep suspicion, or an acute taste for things piquant and acidic.

In the *Guide Culinaire*, the scallop was designated to a bath of oil, lemon and parsley for half-an-hour, before frying and serving with one of the stronger hollandaise sauces such as béarnaise or tartar. Curried, Newburg, drowned in cream and gin, all seem guises designed for times when the scallop might be understudying something else, or used as padding. Or perhaps these bullish techniques are just a mark of how modern tastes have been brutalized by chemical additives.

After what appears to have been many decades of soul searching, one thesis emerged that convinced most kitchens, and which became so common that menus would only say *coquilles St Jacques*.

Two recipes are combined. Parisienne uses mushrooms in the cooking liquor to stretch out the scallop. The sauce is a plainer wine base. The other is mornay, properly Gruyère and Parmesan in place of the mushrooms. The top might have been dusted with breadcrumbs to create a good crust. For a time, the scallop knew no other burial.

COQUILLES ST JACQUES

THE FISH: Scrub the scallop shells. Put them, rounded side down, in a low oven to open. Remove, and cut out the white flesh. Reserve the coral. Blanch the meat in a white wine courtbouillon with onion, mushroom, thyme and bay.

THE SAUCE: Wash out the scallop shell. Pipe around the edge a border of *pommes duchesse* (baked mashed potato, mixed with 4 egg yolks to 1 white). Fill the shell with a flour-based sauce: either white wine or mornay. Lay the scallops on top. Bake and then glaze under the salamander before serving.

Such militant procedures rely on the textural contrast of the scallops' thick, silken flesh and the smoothness of the flour-based sauce, against the flouriness of the potatoes: a homage in off-whites. The corals would have been destroyed in the poaching and grilling, and would never have achieved the fullness they can with light pan frying or grilling. But in America the corals remain under suspicion, and are rarely used.

When the modern kitchen finally broke away from this dogma, it strode down another blind alley, this time of mousses and purées. This was often as extravagant a misuse, or, perhaps, a means of making use of a surfeit. The scallop was reduced to a role only for its sweetness, or as a mirror to other, more expensive, fish.

Executed properly, as in this example from the Savoy under Anton Edelmann's regime, it was transformed into something totally different. If hiding away a stuffing inside was a classical introversion, here at least was regal mitigation.

SCALLOP MOUSSE WITH CAVIAR AFTER ANTON EDELMANN

THE MOUSSE: Wash and dry 2 parts of white scallop, to 1 part sole. Season. Cool in the fridge for at least ½ hour. Mince. Set a bowl on ice and pass the minced fish through a sieve into it. For each 4oz fish, add an equal quantity of cream, 1 egg white and ½ yolk. Chill until firm.

THE COOKING: Spoon the mixture into buttered ramekins, putting a filling of caviar in the centre. Cover. Wrap in cling film. Steam 8 minutes.

THE BEURRE BLANC: Reduce shallot, peppercorns, white wine and vinegar. Cream. Work in the butter, a piece at a time. Season with cayenne. Garnish with caviar.

If that recipe now seems like a half-way house, or a hat-tipping to the Savoy's place in the classical peerage, the modern kitchen has been more prepared to show off the fish for itself. Sometimes this has been as simplistic as a quick pan fry, serving on a mix of lettuces as a warm salad. Good white wines, especially the sweeter ones such as Barsac and Sauternes, repay their investment in the poaching, and go on to provide magisterial bases for other fish sauces. Both these dishes are essentially variations on a *beurre blanc*, in which the scallop has become central.

SCALLOP SALAD

THE SALAD: Scrape and cut carrots and Jerusalem artichokes to equal lengths and thicknesses. Steam. Cut French beans to the same length. Cut the scallops into sections slightly larger than the vegetables.

THE COOKING: Dice a shallot. Sweat in a little butter. Season with vinegar. Add the scallops and vegetables. Sauté lightly. Add a glass of white wine to cook and deglaze as the fish and vegetables cook. Take out the scallops as the liquid reaches a simmer, and let the vegetables cook on for another couple of minutes.

The same idea works the other way round.

SCALLOP RAGOÛT

THE VEGETABLES: Cut to equal size 3 or 4 vegetables chosen for their different qualities of colour and texture – a root, a green, an aromatic – and par-boil any that will need more cooking than the scallop.

THE COOKING: Sweat a shallot in butter. Add wine and a little fish stock. Simmer. Reduce a little. Add the vegetables and the scallops. Simmer for 5–6 minutes, depending on the thickness of the vegetables and the scallops. Grill the corals separately. Take out the fish and vegetables and plate them. Reduce the sauce at a swift boil. Mount with butter as for hollandaise, and pour over the ragoût.

Cantonese restaurants arrived at a simpler, but direct, approach. All the inessentials have been cast aside. The sauce is just the juices from the steaming, infused with the garlic and the scallop. A second side sauce of spring onions, over which a mix of boiling soy flavoured with ginger and chilli has been poured, is usually offered as well. The Chinese say it adds zest, though it can upset the balance.

STEAMED SCALLOPS CANTONESE STYLE

THE SEASONING: Heat a wok with oil until it starts to smoke, and then quickly deep fry some diced garlic until the skin starts to brown. Take out the garlic and lay it on top of the scallop, along with some diced spring onion.

THE SCALLOPS: Place the scallops in their shells in a steamer, cover, and steam over a high heat for about 8 minutes.

The Cantonese are free with scallops. A variation is to slip a knife into the centre, and stuff the middle with a prawn paste. Scallops liberally grace stir-fries, where they can take on the tastes of the other ingredients, especially the more exotic elements like wild mushrooms or even oysters. Something of the same thinking might be found in this buttery dish.

STIR-FRIED SCALLOPS
WITH CABBAGE AND TARRAGON

THE CABBAGE: Shred the cabbage. Par-boil briefly. Take out and squeeze dry.

THE SCALLOPS: Pan fry the scallops briefly to brown the outsides.

THE COOKING: Add a good measure of butter to the scallops and stir-fry in the cabbage to absorb the extra butter. Add the chopped tarragon. Take out the scallops and the cabbage. Deglaze the pan with a little wine and pour over the scallops and cabbage.

Allying fish and meat is a fragile frontier, but there are examples of successful dishes. The Cantonese use Yunnan ham to season the flesh of thick fish; trout and bacon is an English example; more extravagantly, lamb with crab is surprisingly successful, and with scallops slightly less so. But using veal stock to sauce the scallops provides the opportunity to drink red wine with fish.

Jean-Louis Dumonet comes from a restaurant family. His father has a bistro in Paris, he trained with Louis Outhier, working for a while at Ninety Park Lane, and now has his own restaurant at Châteauroux with his Scottish wife.

COQUILLES ST JACQUES RÔTIES AU JUS DE VIANDE

THE POTATOES: Put some butter in a little cake tin. Grate and dry 1 big Rosevald potato. Pack the potato into the tin, and cook briefly on both sides to brown.

THE SAUCE: Liaise a first-class brown veal stock with a little flour. Reduce, and mount with butter as for hollandaise.

THE SCALLOPS: Cut 3 scallops in half and pan fry for 2 minutes, on 1 side only. Season them well after they are cooked.

TO SERVE: Put the potato cake in the middle of the plate. Arrange the scallops around it to overlap. Deglaze the pan with the veal stock and mount with butter. Pour around the scallops.

SEA BASS: THE NEW PRETENDER

SO MANY CHINESE restaurants opened or upgraded in the early Eighties, that the price of seabass spiralled. From minority billing, with only a generic mention in the *Guide Culinaire*, it came back into vogue, cross-fertilizing from immigrant cooking to European. The Cantonese wanted it for one dish:

STEAMED SEABASS WITH GINGER
AND SPRING ONIONS

THE FISH: Slash the sides of the washed fish at the fattest points. Lay the whole fish on a steamer. Turn the heat right up. Cover. Cook for about 10 minutes.

THE SAUCE: In a separate pan, heat some good oil. Chop ginger and spring onions into shards, and pass briefly through the oil. Add soy sauce. Pour over the fish to serve.

The saucing is disarmingly simple and direct, but this was a recipe designed for other thick-fleshed fish, like the grouper found in the South China Seas. Another lift for the seabass' reputation was Paul Bocuse's dish, *en croute* with a lobster mousse and served with a sauce Choron.

Brian Turner, once head chef of London's Capital Hotel and now in his own restaurant, Turner's, a few blocks away, puts a more modern interpretation to it. The fish is either pan fried, in which case it is cut as medallions; or roasted, when the fillet is used. The sauce is sometimes based on a crab stock made from the shells and spiked with tarragon. Caramelizing the cabbage echoes the batters and crusts of less precise cookings.

SEABASS WITH RED CABBAGE

THE CABBAGE: Shred a red cabbage. Simmer slowly in red wine and veal stock with *crème de cassis*. Set aside. On ordering, take portion of cabbage and place in the roasting oven so the sugars caramelize and the cabbage is crisp.

THE SAUCE: Mix ½ pint fish stock, ¼ pint Noilly Prat and ¼ pint veal stock with a crushed garlic clove and 1 teaspoon chopped shallot. Reduce by two-thirds. Add ½ pint double cream and reduce to thicken.

THE FISH: Cut three incisions in a 6oz fillet of bass, with the skin on. Heat 2oz butter in a pan and seal the flesh side, flip over and cook gently for 10 minutes until crisp.

TO SERVE: Place the fillet on the cabbage, surround with the sauce and garnish with dill.

OTHER FISH: THE HANDING ON OF TRADITIONS

WITH OTHER FISH the sequences have been less marked. However, sole normande is so much a part of the northern French tradition, that it is heartening to find the southern coast ports of England with similar dairy agriculture and access to the same fishing waters, not completely devoid of effective recipes. This one is credited to Devon.

JOHN DORY WITH CIDER

THE FISH: Cut the fish, on the bone, into steaks. Warm butter in a pan and sauté the steaks. Wet with a glass of cider, and season with lemon. Poach gently.

THE SAUCE: Take out the fish. Deglaze the pan with cream. Pour over the fish.

MONKFISH

The tail of the monkfish is a thick fillet. Its reputation has been one of secrecy and surreptitiousness. As a fisherman itself, it is sometimes called anglerfish because its giant mouth gapes wide for any innocent fish to swim into, when it will snap shut. In the classical kitchen it was often used as a substitute for lobster or scampi, disguised in a cream sauce. The flesh seems to have more affinity with the terrestrial, gutsy flavours of meat cookery than with the leaner, fish stock and cream mix, that suits thinner, frailer fish. This dish, from the first of Keith Floyd's books, reeks of Provence, but might as well have been for lamb, or even veal.

ROAST MONKFISH WITH GARLIC AFTER
KEITH FLOYD

THE FISH: Skin the tail, and make a few short incisions along the back and sides. Into these, slip slices of peeled garlic. Brown the fish in hot oil. Season with salt, pepper, thyme, fennel and lemon. Add the rest of the bulb of garlic, unpeeled. Roast in a hot oven for about 20 minutes. Serve with grilled tomatoes.

Similarly, this braise, where the tail is lifted off the floor of the pan with a bed of herbs, and the wine is red, not white.

MONKFISH BRAISED WITH RED WINE

THE FISH: Cut the tail into steaks. Chop parsley and chives, and lay the steaks on the herbs. Moisten with a glass of red wine. Cook in the oven. Take out the fillets. Finish with a little cream.

Jane Grigson points out in *Fish Cookery* that sauce Americaine is one of the best accompaniments to monkfish. This sauce is from Provence, but has been augmented, through restaurant use, with lobster, as credited to Noel Peters in Paris in the mid-1850s. Arguably monk, with its thick flesh, is even better suited. Two stages of cooking allow sauce and fish to fuse.

MONKFISH AMERICAINE

THE FISH: Sweat onions, garlic and shallot until they start to colour. Wipe the monkfish tail in a seasoned flour and brown lightly with the onions. Flame with brandy. Take out the monkfish and set aside. Chop tomatoes and herbs and add to the onions. Deglaze with white wine. Season with wine vinegar and sugar. Cook slowly until the liquid has almost disappeared, perhaps 20 minutes. Place the monkfish back in the pan and cook slowly for 10–15 minutes.

TO SERVE: Take out the fillet and carve. Lay on the sauce, which should by now be almost a paste.

SALTING

Salt fish went out of fashion in Britain with the arrival of the railways. Before then, it was a common way of preserving the catch. In some port areas it was a staple food. In the Highlands cod were lain out on the rocks to dry, while in Bristol it was an early export, going out on the boats which were to bring back port. In better-off families, salt fish was for Ash Wednesday and Good Friday, served with mashed parsnips. Alastair Little, a keen exponent of market cooking, using the full range of the cosmopolitan Soho larder, revives the technique to give a new slant to an ordinary dish.

SALT COD WITH MASHED POTATOES
AFTER ALASTAIR LITTLE

THE FISH: Pack a fresh fillet of cod in sea salt. Cover. Leave in the fridge at least 2 days. It will keep a few weeks. Take out the fillet and rinse off under a cold running tap for 24 hours.

THE COOKING: Cut the fillet into steaks. Steam. Serve with mashed potatoes mixed with butter and olive oil, and a green vegetable.

THE CONTINENTAL STYLE

In England, the collapse of the indigenous agriculture through war, rationing and austerity, gave birth to a hybrid of a restaurant which mixed some of the Edwardian splendour of earlier dining rooms with imported cookings. The Continental restaurant was a strange mix of the pragmatic and the exotic. The White Tower opened in 1938, and is still run by the Stais family. The cooking takes its lead from Greece but with more than a few nods towards the classical kitchen. The menu, though, is an elegant piece of gastronomic literature, appropriately so, as the Tower has always been a haunt of the publishing glitterati from nearby Bedford Square.

FISH SALAD AFTER THE WHITE TOWER

'It is not always the most complicated and rich sauce that makes the tastiest dish. The secret of the appetizing freshness of this salad is that it is dressed while still warm, and must be eaten soon afterwards. For this reason we make it twice a day, and only in small quantities.

'One day I saw my old chef smacking his chops with an ethereal expression on his fat chubby face, which told me as clearly that he was enjoying something out of this world. I asked him what it was that evidently gave him so much pleasure and he replied: "Nothing much, Guv'nor – just a little salad I made with the turbot trimmings, some raw onion, parsley, lemon and olive oil. My mother used to make it and was very fond of it. Try a little, it's very nice. You'll like it." I did . . . a new star joined the White Tower firmament.'

The era of the White Tower was also the era of The Bell at Aston Clinton, an old coaching inn on the Aylesbury to London road. Gerard Harris gave up the law to turn it into one of the foremost restaurants of the post-war era. But even in the early Sixties, the menu was stamped in the classical French tradition of *coq au vin 3/6d, sweetbreads chasseur 8/6d, entrecote marchand de vin 11/-, pheasant smitane, woodcock flambée*. Smokies in cream were added to the repertoire in 1955, after Harris took a break in Arbroath. They are still there.

SMOKING

The smokie is a hot-smoked haddock. The fish is salted, and then slow smoked over a fire of oak chips, so it is at once partially preserved in the fumes and partially cooked. The only cooking it needs is to be warmed through under a grill and then flaked on to hot buttered toast. Smokies originate from the tiny fishing village of Auchmithie, a cluster of white-washed cottages on the banks of a steep-sided bay, from where the first settlers, probably from Scandinavia, fished the north sea in long, narrow row boats. Eventually, their prowess led them to be headhunted by the burghers of Arbroath with offers of new houses, bigger boats and commercial smokeries in place of their living-room chimneys.

BELL INN SMOKIES

Butter a small ramekin. Put a teaspoon of tomato concasse in the bottom. Flake the fish and fill the ramekin. Top up with Jersey cream. Top with Parmesan. Bake until the surface browns.

ENGLAND MEETS FRANCE

Langan's Brasserie, on the site of the Coq d'Or, was the epicentre of fashionable London for the Seventies and Eighties under the triumvirate of Michael Caine, the late Peter Langan and the man who kept the show on the road, Richard Shepherd. The cooking was rarely at the front of fashion, staying loyal to English dishes and the best kind of pre-*nouvelle* cooking. For this dish, which has become a signature on the menu, Shepherd somehow manages to fuse the old Englishness of the anchovies, with an otherwise solidly French attack.

SOUFFLÉ AUX ÉPINARDS, SAUCE ANCHOIS
AFTER RICHARD SHEPHERD

THE SOUFFLÉ: Make a white sauce with 2½oz butter, 2½oz flour, 1 pint milk. Season with cayenne, nutmeg and salt. Add 4 egg yolks and 4oz spinach, lightly cooked only, or it will lose its greenness. Beat the whites from the eggs until stiff and fold into the mix. Spoon out on to half-a-dozen buttered moulds, and bake at gas 4, 350°F (180°C) for 20 minutes.

THE SAUCE: Pound a small tin of anchovies to a paste. In a bain-marie over hot water, whisk 2 egg yolks with 1 tablespoon water. Cool slightly. Slowly, add 8oz melted butter, whisking all the time. Season with lemon. Whisk in the anchovy paste.

TO SERVE: Pierce the top of the soufflé at table, and pour the sauce into the heart of the soufflé.

LONDON, 1953 · SOHO AND THE WEST END

The major restaurants listed in the second edition of the *Good Food Guide* divided between classical French and the London tradition of shellfish and oyster bars.

SHELLFISH AND OYSTERS

BENTLEYS
'Oyster stew 10/-
turtle soup 3/-.'

DRIVER'S
'For many years it has been traditional to go if you are looking for oysters, shellfish or indeed any fish of first class quality.'

GARRICK HOTEL
'Now that the Café Royal has changed so much, the ghosts of the nineties rest here.'

OVERTON'S
'For 80 years famous as an oyster bar and fish restaurant.' Opened in 1872 by Horace Overton.

RULES
'For about a century this has been the tavern for artists and writers.'

SCOTT'S
'Known for a great many years as an excellent place for fish and all seafoods.'

WHEELER'S
'There are some who hold, soundly, that this is the best place for fish . . . the bisque d'homard (lobster stock, cream and brandy) is splendid.'

WILTON'S
'One of the smaller, more distinguished and more expensive restaurants dependent upon an oyster business.'

CLASSICAL FRENCH

BOULESTIN

'The shadow of a great name, that of X. M. Boulestin, covers this restaurant . . . poussin au champagne, truite gastronome.'

CAFÉ ROYAL

'Where is Oscar? Where is Bosie? Nothing returns.'

CAPRICE

'Ambience and haute cuisine.'

CHEZ VICTOR

'French cooking done as it should be.'

CONNAUGHT

'Three genuine specialities in the sense that they are probably unique: crêpes de volaille Connaught; sole Carlos; oeufs poché en surprise.'

COQ D'OR

'Go when you feel rich and don't care what you pay.' NB: Now Langan's Brasserie.

ESCARGOT BIENVENU

'Outside, a sign showing a sleek and probably luscious snail; inside a rapid fire of French conversation between members of staff.'

ETOILE

'I shall live here when I win Littlewoods.'

KETTNERS

'Sole bonne femme 4/6; sole Juive – a large Dover sole fried to order in olive oil and served with grated beetroot and horseradish.'

LA BELLE MEUNIÈRE

'Good French cooking from a large and rather confusing menu.'

L'EPICURE

'A new restaurant, as yet without a licence, but drinks fetched at reasonable prices.'

MIRABELLE

'Luxury cuisine in luxury surroundings . . . Duck with cherries or olives done very well.'

MON PLAISIR

'Simple French cooking.' NB: still open.

PRUNIER'S

'Bouillabaisse 9/6, poisson St James (white fish in white wine and curry sauce) 6/6.'

WHITE'S HOTEL

'Specialities include vol au vent Toulousiane, caneton sauvage à l'orange.'

THE DROVE ROADS

—

MEAT COOKING

ROAST BEEF OF OLD ENGLAND

THE NORTHERN MOORS were the stock-breeding areas of the middle ages. The lairds and the church owned vast tracts of grazing land. Cattle were a rich man's business. In a poor family, the ox took preference and was given hay and corn so it was fit to plough in the spring.

By high summer, traffic on the drove roads south began to build up. Much of the early cross-breeding took place as the cattle were moved to the urban markets. Inns and taverns tended to be sited close to stop-over points, where there was grazing. Innkeepers took animals from the herd for roasting, out of which grew the tradition of English roast beef.

Horseradish came into play with beef, partly for medical reasons. It was used as an embrocation for people and animals, or to clear heads. It was grown by taverns and at port and river landing stages, where it was used as a quick cure for sea sickness.

Its first introduction was as shavings, like truffles, peeled thinly over the beef, or else a seasoning for cream or in a form of porridge with milk and oatmeal. This would have been a fundamental native seasoning and, by the time of the *Guide*, had been formalized into sauces like sauce Albert, or canapés: black bread spread with mustard and chopped chives, diced horseradish and chopped, hard-boiled egg.

The Aberdeen Angus was developed by Hugh Watson of Keillor near Dundee, an area otherwise known for its toffee and, lately, its berries. The Angus was first shown in 1820. Watson butchered his own carcasses, and sent them on the newly opened railways to London. Before the railways, drovers preferred hornless cattle for the good reasons that they were more manageable and less likely to gore each other or the drovers on the long roads south to the Norfolk marshes, where they were fattened off, ready for markets in the Midlands and London.

THE NEED FOR HANGING

Scottish beef's reputation, and the reputation of the English as meat-eaters, stemmed from these annual drives. But they also depended on two factors that no longer play any part. The meat was cooked in larger joints, which made it more flavoursome. And it was hung. By design, and for practical reasons, the meat might have been kept for eight weeks and more, especially in winter, and certainly for longer than the ten days to two weeks that count as hanging now. The French term *mortification* suggests the meat might well have been quite rotten and decayed outside. This might go some way to explaining the taste for spicy condiments. Other evidence that this long process of putrefaction was actively encouraged, comes from the Argentinian gauchos, who also breed Aberdeen Angus strains, and, so the machismo has it, hang joints from the ceiling and only take it for cooking when the flesh falls off the hook.

The supermarkets stopped meat being hung. It was too expensive to keep meat in store. Carcasses arrive the day after slaughtering, and are now butchered straightaway. The bright, wet, red, almost rosy, hues of the chill cabinet, are at the other end of the spectrum to the nineteenth century idea of quality, which was meat that was dirty brown, dry, with thick fingers of fat running through the middle.

MARINATION

The early kitchen had other ways of preserving meat. Marination also served to tenderize meat which, before modern quality control, would have been more worrying for the kitchen, especially if they were buying from drovers who passed through only once or twice a year. This recipe is from Bristol, and bears the unmistakable stamp of the trade with Oporto. Worcester sauce is a latter day substitute for something more piquant like a catsup, or even a *verjus*.

STEAK WITH SHERRY (TRADITIONAL)

THE STEAK: Marinate a rump or sirloin steak in sherry and pepper for 3 hours. Take out. Pat dry. Melt some butter in a pan. Add the steak and some mushrooms. Turn once or twice. Take out the steak and keep warm.

THE SAUCE: Deglaze the frying pan with the marinade, Worcester sauce and herbs. Reduce and finish with cream.

Marinades took on the complexity of stock-making. Wines were seasoned with onions, shallots, celery, thyme, bay, parsley, garlic, peppercorns; sometimes sweated off in oil first, sometimes macerated raw in the wine. It was only the arrival of refrigeration that closed down this department, and pushed the device into another direction as simple seasoning.

Gary Rhodes, at the county-town hotel the Castle, in Taunton, uses seasonings from the modern era, Asian, rather than European, to pull off this dish.

MARINATED FILLET OF BEEF WITH SOY AND CORIANDER AFTER GARY RHODES

THE MARINADE: Make up a generous marinade, enough to bathe the beef, with soy sauce seasoned with Worcester sauce, mushroom ketchup, olive oil. Mix in crushed coriander seeds, fresh coriander leaves, garlic, honey, chilli pepper and allspice. Place the whole fillet of beef in the marinade and leave in the fridge for 3–4 days, turning regularly.

1. Roasted: Heat a pan and sauté-roast the wiped fillet on top of the stove, so the inside is still blue. Take out the beef. Deglaze the pan with the macerated groundnut oil and a little of the marinade.

TO SERVE: Slice the beef. Arrange a salad in a warm bowl and dress lightly with the deglazed marinade. Arrange the beef around the salad and serve with more of the marinade and groundnut oil as a sauce.

2. As carpaccio: Take out the fillet and wipe dry. Slice thinly and arrange to cover the plate. Dress with black pepper, a smear of macerated oil (in the hotel, this is a dressing without vinegar using groundnut oil macerated with shallots, garlic, fresh herbs and a little olive oil for three days), and shavings of fresh Parmesan.

STEAKS

The steak came to be the restaurant's way of serving beef, an easily manageable portion, distinct from the communal carveries of the early inns.

For Escoffier and the classical kitchen, the prime steak was the thin end of the fillet cut into one-and-a-half-inch slices weighing about four ounces: the tournedos. More than 100 recipes in the *Guide* read like an atlas: Andalouse (with chipolatas and aubergine), Baltimore (with creamed maize), Catalane (with tomato and pepper), Japonais (on croquettes with Japanese artichokes), Mexicaine (on a grilled mushroom with tomato purée); and a who-was-who: Belle-Helene (on a bed of asparagus), Benjamin (with potatoes and stuffed mushrooms), Helder (with béarnaise and tomato purée), Lili (on a cake of pommes anna with artichokes and foie gras), Rachel (with artichokes and bone marrow). Most famous of all was Rossini, created by Escoffier for the composer.

TOURNEDOS ROSSINI AFTER ESCOFFIER

THE STEAK: Season the tournedos and shallow fry in butter. Lay on a croûton fried in clarified butter and coated with a little meat glaze. Fry a slice of foie gras, and lay over the fillet. Place a thick slice of truffle on top.

THE SAUCE: Deglaze the pan with Madeira, add a little demi-glace flavoured with truffle. Strain and pour over the steak.

For contrast, Escoffier also gave the recipe for his grandmother's version:

Pan fry a rump steak in butter. Add half-cooked potatoes cut into ovals, glazed button onions and batons of bacon. Plate the steak, onions and potatoes and deglaze the pan with bouillon. Add a few drops lemon juice, garnish with parsley.

Fernand Point gave a rather less refined version of what he termed Fisherman's beef, which comes from the bargees on the Rhône.

FISHERMAN'S BEEF AFTER FERNAND POINT

Brown the beef in oil in a pan. Remove. Dice a shallot. Simmer in a glass of red wine vinegar, and 1 of white wine. Add tomato purée and caramel. Cook 15 minutes. Add the beef. Mix flour and water into a roux and add to the sauce. Cook 30 minutes.

The Champany Inn at Linlithgow, an old horse mill converted by a South African butcher Clive Davidson and his wife Anne into the premier steak restaurant in Scotland, favour a Scots Blue Cross ahead of Angus.

Davidson holds that the beef should glisten. The fat should be cream-coloured and flake off when scraped with a nail. And the animal should have had to work for his meals: too early in the year and the cattle are gorged on the soft young grass. By July, they are having to fight harder for the short, drier tufts.

The meat is hung in a chill room for four to eight weeks. Ionizers inhibit the mould growth and keep the weight loss down to around ten per cent.

Steaks are thick cut, at least an inch-and-a-half, painted with olive oil to stop the outside burning, and cooked across a gas-fired lava rock grill, that has been on for at least an hour. They are turned once or twice, but not more, or the meat toughens.

THE GREAT DIVIDE

The way British and French cooks handle beef, provides a simple snapshot of national differences. In France, the meat was pot-roasted, slow-cooked, the nutritional value spread out over a week, the meat probably tough and in need of tenderizing. In Britain, the meat was dry-roasted, served with side relishes, made to go further with other dishes that could be brought to the table at the same time. The one essentially a domestic process, the other an external cooking, done in cookshops and taverns and perhaps brought back to the family; the one arguably rural, the other urban.

Point made this dish for a fellow restaurateur Marius Guillet, owner of a Lyons bistro Le Mal Assis. It is a culture away from roast beef:

PIÈCE DE BOEUF À LA ROYALE

Interlard a top beef rump with strips of pork fat and ham. Tie up, and put in a large braising pan with onions, carrots. Brown all 3 evenly in oil. Flambé with cognac. Add a bottle of champagne, and enough beef stock to cover. Add 3 blanched calves' feet, pork fat, tomatoes and garlic. Add herbs and seasoning after the boil. Seal up hermetically, and cook in a moderate oven for 2½ hours. Take out the beef and strain the stock, twice, if necessary, to ensure it is clean, then pour it back over the beef in a second, smaller braising pot and cook again for 1½ hours, basting frequently. Drain carefully so that it keeps it shape without breaking, and place in an oval terrine of about the same size. Cover with the juice, which will by now be a jelly, and refrigerate for a day. Serve cold with a salad and a Côtes du Rhône.

Behind this lies a deeper divide, not just of butchery techniques, but also of husbanding. The cattle were different. Aberdeen Angus and other breeds, like Hereford, are fattier. The fat is a lubricant in the cooking. The leaner, larger, more fibrous Charolais of France or Belgian Blue were designed for the pot. Even a fillet of Charolais might be consigned to the pot, with onions, tomatoes and herbs, covered and cooked in a low oven. Such a fate seems unnecessary for a fillet from a Hereford, which, if hung for two weeks or more, can be tender enough to cut with the side of a fork.

English cooks seasoned the plate, rather than the pot or pan. A fillet might have been roasted, left to cool and served on a summer evening cold, rolled in freshly cut herbs or with a mayonnaise spiked with anchovies.

Beef has come to its regal position at the head of the culinary table because it has the force of presence to live with all manner of flavours without being subdued by them: rosemary, oysters, blue cheese butters, light smoking, horseradish, mustard.

And, most notoriously, pepper.

STEAK AU POIVRE (TRADITIONAL)

Grind two tablespoons of spicy pepper on to a plate, and wipe the fillet steaks across them. Sauté the steaks at a good pace. Flambé with cognac. Take out the steaks and reserve in a warm pan. Deglaze with Madeira. Strain. Add cream.

In more modern mode, there are echoes of Escoffier's walnut sauce for large whole fish in this interpretation from Paul Gayler of Inigo Jones in Covent Garden.

VEAL WITH CAPERS AND WALNUTS AFTER PAUL GAYLER

THE WALNUTS: Shell and blanch the walnuts to skin. Poach in milk. Reserve a few, and purée the rest.

THE SAUCE: Sweat shallots and garlic. Deglaze with white wine. Add capers, veal stock. Reduce by half. Add double cream, and reduce to the colour of white coffee. Finish with the purée of walnuts, butter, some diced walnuts and capers.

THE VEAL: Pan fry the escalope. Garnish with deep fried sweetbreads or calves' brains.

MUTTON: THE FIRST MEAT

HOLLYWOOD TURNED THE American cattle drives into faction, but centuries earlier in Europe, sheep and geese would have been the main drives.

Unlike cattle, sheep are probably native. The wool trade was known to the Romans. By the middle ages, the export of fleeces to Flanders was one of the mainstays of the economy. By 1100 there were seven-and-a-half million sheep in Britain. They were kept by abbeys, manors and by cottagers. Villages employed a shepherd to look after the communal flock. This was a respected job, and he was excused other feudal duties. The meat was only a by-product. Fleeces and milk were more important.

CURES

Ewes were kept for four or five seasons, perhaps even longer. When they were finally slaughtered the meat was spiced and salted, known as

LONDON, 1963 • THREE- AND TWO-STAR RESTAURANTS FROM EGON RONAY

Despite some tipping of the hat towards ethnic cooking, nine out of the top twelve London restaurants in the 1963 *Egon Ronay Guide* remained French. Three out of the top four still followed Escoffier's codes. Parkes was an individualist restaurant in a cramped basement in Beauchamp Place, opened by Ray Parkes, a student of architecture who preferred a more country approach. Only the Savoy or the Jardin des Gourmets survive in anything like the same form today.

THREE STARS	
Coq d'Or	Prunier's
Mirabelle	Caprice
Parkes	Jamshid
Savoy	Young's Chinese Restaurant
	Chez Ciccio
TWO STARS	
Au Jardin des Gourmets	Le Provençal
Hostaria Romana	

---

powdering, and made into hams. This was common food, eaten more than either pork or the occasional luxuries like venison or goat, which also went to hams.

These were wet cures, usually done in cold weather and finished by mild smoking, and produced dry, flat-pressed, compact meats. The legs were rubbed with saltpetre, and left at least a day. A cure was made up of salt and clean water, and the ham put in it for a week. It was then taken out and left to hang in the airy corner of the chimney or up among the rafters to dry for another three weeks. A commercial version appears in *The Art and Mystery of Curing, Preserving and Potting*, 1864.

Rub a leg of mutton with hot treacle, and leave for a day. Make a cure of thyme, marjoram, bay, saltpetre, black pepper boiled in about 5 pints of water for an hour. Cool. Pour over the leg. Leave for 3 weeks, turning daily. Take out the hams, rub dry and wash well with vinegar. Hang to dry. Coat with bran or oatmeal and smoke over a fire of 2 parts oak sawdust, 1 part peat, 2 parts beech, 1 part turfs or fern, for 3 weeks or more. Store in malt cooms of pulverised charcoal for 3 months to mature.

The American preference for cattle over sheep might, it is argued, have been down to the familiarity of mutton in a poor man's diet.

MUTTON IN THE POT

A clear idea of how older animals were treated in everyday use at the end of the last century, is evoked by Dorothy Hartley. The pot was still the main cooking method. '*Nurse took a thick iron pot, and rubbed the bottom inside well with the fat tail of a mutton chop (the point being that she did not want it to burn). She then fetched a scraggy, bloody end of a sheep's neck and, laying it on the stone (not pottery) sink, she chopped it up with an axe and put the pieces in the pot, together with a bunch of bacon rinds plaited together. This pot she now hung on the hook over the fire, and fetched some vegetables from the outhouse. Onions (shallots) were skinned and cut in two and added, and some washed turnip, sliced. Then a small bundle was made up of wiry thyme, a sprig of green mint, a twig of marjoram, and the brown paper peels from the onions; this was tied tightly with twine, and secured to the handle of the pot, hanging the bunch inside. Then the kettle that hung alongside the pot was tilted up and some water poured in (warm, to prevent the cracking of the iron pot), and the whole filled up with cold water. When it boiled, she skimmed the dark scum off very carefully, and replaced the lid until dinner time.*

'*A scoopful was poured into a basin, and a brittle yard of West Riding oatcake was lifted from the rack overhead; a spoon and plate were set at the wooden table by the window and dinner was served.*

'*Curiously, it was not greasy; I expect the meat was so lean and the slight fat from the bacon rinds so thin, that the short preliminary cooking used it up. There was a velvety sheen on the surface, and the yellow skins had given the broth a golden colour. Next day, after it had gone cold, it was skimmed and barley added, but this was definitely another dish, having barley and bits of meat and vegetables in it, and needing a soup plate to eat it in. The first day's boiling was plain broth.*'

In the inns and taverns, mutton would have been roasted. But the mental picture of a group of travellers sitting down to a communal table of roast meats may not always be accurate. This recipe, named after a well-known

Victorian London pub, gives a different idea of how it might have been handled. The meat was sometimes swapped for venison. If the mutton was hot, it was laid on the bread so the juices seeped through.

ALDERMAN'S WALK

Mix chives, Worcester sauce, mustard, tabasco, salt and pepper in a pan with butter. Cut a slice of roast lamb and a slice of bread to equal sizes. Lay the lamb in the sauce. Toast the bread. Lay the lamb over the toasted bread and cover with the sauce.

Early kitchens were not timid about mixing mutton with strong flavours of whatever happened to be in season or in stock. This is a west country recipe for October.

SADDLE OF LAMB WITH APPLE

Rub the inside of a saddle with lemon. Stuff with a mix of diced apples spiced with cloves. Roll up. Rub the outside with ginger and salt. Roast. Baste with cider. Pour off the fat and make a gravy with cider.

AN OUTRAGEOUS PANOPLY

Alexis Soyer's celebrated lamb chops Reform, created while he was working at the Reform Club in the first half of the nineteenth century, now seems an outrageous panoply of mismatched flavours, a dish designed for a different beast, different appetites and different values: the chops battered with a mix of breadcrumbs, ham, tongue and parsley; the sweet and sour sauce of vinegar, sugar, onions, peppers filled out with stock and redcurrant jelly; the whole thing garnished with beets, tongue, hard-boiled eggs and gherkins, the point being to echo the club's colours of red, green and white.

Boiled mutton, with a caper sauce made with the milk stock in which the lamb has cooked, flour and butter, seems a more fitting epitaph to that era of British cookery. But Carême was defensive of the English way. In his nobly titled *Traite des Grosses Pièces de Mutton*, he declares: 'It is a strange error on the part of many chefs to conclude that English gourmets will eat this leg only if served with boiled carrots and turnips. What the English like best is to see the juice coming from the leg when they slice it.'

LEG OF MUTTON À LA BORDELAISE
AFTER CARÊME

THE MEAT: Bone a well-hung leg of mutton. Stuff with ham, anchovies rinsed of all their salt, chopped parsley, shallot and garlic. Tie up to keep the stuffing in. Brown lightly in butter. Moisten with a good bottle of claret. Add carrots, onions, bouquet garni and cook partly covered, slowly, for 1½ hours so the liquid reduces.

THE GARLIC: Lightly boil skinned garlic, then fry in butter and keep hot.

TO SERVE: Take out the leg, reduce the stock, and add a little espagnol. Dress the garlic with a sauce allemande, and serve in a sauceboat.

LEG OF MUTTON À L'ANGLAISE
AFTER ESCOFFIER

THE MEAT: Wrap the leg in a buttered and floured cloth. Plunge into boiling salt water. Add carrots, garlic, onions and bouquet garnis. Tie up a dozen quartered turnips in a cloth and add to the stock. Cook 30 minutes to the pound.

TO SERVE: Purée the turnips. Make a butter sauce with the stock and 3 tablespoons capers. Skim and strain stock, and serve separately.

TRADITIONAL BREEDS

Such early recipes are hard to envisage, because the animals themselves were so different. We have come to think of lamb as if it were a single, standard item. Supermarkets and recipe books have persuaded us that this is possible. But what classifies as mutton, might not even pass the quality standard. Even fifty years ago, let alone 100 or 200 years, the skill of the kitchen was to deal with the vagaries of different breeds, and the different ages at which they had been slaughtered. A Shropshire or Leicestershire animal was too fat, and the cooking became greasy. Mountain animals did not provide enough fat for cooking. Many of these breeds are now extinct, or close to it.

The downland Oxfords, Hampshires, Dorsets and Shropshires were the mutton of the last century, and survive only with the rare breed collectors. There are still some Romney Marsh sheep in Kent, large-bodied, heavy-coated, hardy, motherly animals that resemble the breeds found in Roman times. They are slow to mature, which does not help their commercial prospects, but thrive on the tough marsh grasses of what is now reclaimed land, and the salty sea air. The Romney Marsh was the great stud of Victorian farming and was exported to Australia, Argentina,

Chile, Uruguay, Peru, Brazil, America, Canada, South Africa, and, most importantly of all, in 1858 to New Zealand.

Other traditional breeds have been phased out altogether: the Lincolnshire Long Wool with its twenty-inch coat; the foraging, courageous, bearded Exmoor Horn that climbs like a goat and will take on animals twice its size; the friendly, deer-like Soay with its curved belly, spindly legs, erect long neck, often kept as a pet. In some cases, as with the long-boned Cotswold, shorn in spring save for a dreadlock clump of wool on its head so its coat could be judged at market, a breed never reached any status in the kitchen. Their role was always to provide wool, and more wool.

Some breeds have made a virtue of their rarity. On the island of North Ronaldsay, the sheep feed on seaweed. They graze on the shoreline, cut off from inland by a dyke. The result is an almost unique animal. The fat is more oily; the flavour strong and salty; the flesh dark, turning grey. Their harsh life and natural configuration mean there is not much meat to bone, and the bones themselves are hard to butcher. They are roasted on a bed of straw with a little stock, and served with a sharp sauce, perhaps of black, red or white currants or berries. But, like the Cotswold, their real merits are probably not culinary.

Other breeds have adapted more successfully. The Herdwick, white-faced, hardy, born with a dark brown or even black wool that turns a blue-grey, gave its shaggy coat for carpet wool. But the meat is dark and luscious.

Early in summer, the medallions cut off the loin are tender enough to be just pan fried for a few minutes. At the Old Vicarage at Witherslack, legs are roasted for an hour-and-three-quarters in a medium oven in August but, by the late autumn, after the animals have grazed that much longer on the unforgiving pastures of the high fells, the cooking has stretched out to three hours in a slightly less hot oven to compensate. The pan juices have been filled up with water to stop the meat drying out. It is served with a jelly of damsons or apple and mint.

LEG OF HERDWICK LAMB AFTER
THE OLD VICARAGE

THE STOCK: Cover some lamb bones, carrots, onion, celery, garlic with water. Simmer 5 hours. Strain. Cool. Skim off the fat.

THE LAMB: Slip slices of garlic and rosemary under the skin of the leg. Place the lamb in an open pot, with enough water just to cover the bottom of the pan. Roast. Top up the water as necessary. 20 minutes from the end of the cooking, pour off all the liquid and turn the meat over to brown. Take out and leave to rest.

THE SAUCE: Add to the roasting juices a cup of the stock, white wine, sherry or Marsala. Reduce to thicken.

Another hill sheep to survive is the small, heavy-coated Welsh mountain sheep, that has managed to keep its role both as a producer of wool and a provider of meat. The flesh is conspicuously tougher than the downland sheep, but is less fatty and has more flavour from its life spent grappling for footholds on the high, slatey inclines.

Traditionally, for fresh meat the chosen joint was a saddle, hung for a week, roasted with the mountain herbs, especially thyme, on which it had grazed. Elsewhere, the hedgerow provided seasoning.

FRUITS AND SEASONINGS

Fruit and herb jellies were a singularly British tack. Although redcurrant is the most common fruit for lamb today, in the past rowan, apple, rhubarb, gooseberry, other currants, even elder have come into play. The salt lamb that grazed on the marshes of the Severn estuary were sent up to fashionable Bath with laver sauce or samphire. Mint sauce was likely to be razor sharp, with the mint just chopped into vinegar and perhaps seasoned with sugar; a gentler version given by Sheila Hutchins is to pound the leaves to a purée, cover with sugar, wet with a little boiling water and then season with lemon. In earlier cookery, mint was even served as a vegetable on its own, steeped in orange juice with a little sugar.

The French tend to use herbs and seasonings on the meat, not to the side. These two variations on a theme have been fixtures of the menu at Chez Moi, an elegant ground-floor restaurant tucked among the imperially large houses on a wide street in Holland Park.

The lamb is Welsh, hung for a week by the butcher and then butchered in the restaurant and kept for a further five or six days. In the French trim, the fat is left on, but Richard Walton cuts it right down in the English way so the best end is just bone and meat. He allows four chops for serving pink, five for people who prefer well-done. The first spring lamb needs nearly half the cooking of the later animals, and even then twelve minutes is in a restaurant oven, which builds up the high temperature and allows the cooking process to freewheel on as the lamb stands after taking out of the oven. At home, in a gentler oven, it will need more cooking. The garlic is not blanched, as is increasingly the vogue in France, but peeled.

RACK OF LAMB AFTER RICHARD WALTON

1. With garlic and mint

THE PASTE: Make a paste of skinned garlic cloves and olive oil in a liquidizer. It should be quite loose and runny to baste the meat. Turn the meat upside down, and separate each chop half-way with a sharp knife. Into each slit, spread the paste. Bruise fresh mint and lay a leaf on the paste between the chops.

THE COOKING: Turn the joint upright. Brush well with butter. Salt. Pepper. Cook for 12 minutes for pink in a hot oven, and leave to rest for 5.

2. With herb crust

THE CRUST: Smear the smooth side of the rack with Dijon mustard. Dice a shallot and set on to the mustard. Mix breadcrumbs, Worcester sauce, black pepper and nutmeg with as many chopped fresh herbs as are to hand. Add butter to get a strong texture. Pack this tightly on to the mustard and shallot coating.

THE COOKING: Roast 12 minutes for pink, and leave to stand 10 minutes to let the cooking finish. To serve, flash under the grill to crisp the crust.

These are country recipes brought from the farmyard to the bistro. By contrast, David Adlard betrays his classical training at the Connaught with this more extended and elaborate series of works. The crust is not added until the lamb is almost cooked. The seasonings are deliberately Provençal.

RACK OF ENGLISH LAMB AFTER DAVID ADLARD

THE LAMB: Chine out the rack of lamb, trim off the excess fat around the nut of the meat, cut the bones 6cm above the nut of the meat and scrape them clean.

THE CRUST: Dice and sweat in 50g butter, 1 shallot and 1 clove garlic. Do not colour. After 3 minutes, add about 20 rosemary spikes, finely chopped, and sweat for 1 minute more. Stir in enough white breadcrumbs to make a paste, but keep the mixture moist.

THE AUBERGINE GÂTEAU: Cut the aubergine into circles 2mm thick. Lay on a tray lined with kitchen paper, and salt lightly. After 45 minutes, pat with paper to absorb the bitter juice. Fry quickly in a pan half-filled with hot oil. Do not brown. Drain. Line four ramekins with the aubergine slices. Half-fill with a thick tomato coulis. Top with plain yoghurt. Fold over the aubergine and cover with foil.

THE SAUCE: Sweat 4 diced shallots for 3 minutes. Add 200ml Madeira and reduce by one-third. Add 500ml lamb glaze. Reduce until syrupy. Season with Meaux mustard and keep warm in a bain-marie.

THE COOKING: Brown the seasoned lamb on top of the stove, and cook in the oven at gas 6, 400°F (200°C) for 10–15 minutes. Press the meat with a finger to test: lots of give – very pink; very resistant – well done. Rest for 20 minutes.

Cover the fat rounded area above the meat with the shallot rosemary mixture. Warm the lamb in the oven for 3 minutes and then put it under the grill to brown the breadcrumbs.

Warm the aubergine in the oven. Turn out on kitchen paper to drain off excess oil. Cut the lamb into chops – 3 per person. Stir 25g unsalted butter into the sauce. Arrange the chops and aubergines on the plate and pour the sauce around.

A variation is this slightly bizarre, but successful, combination from Frances Atkins first at the Old Plough at Speen and then Farleyer House at Aberfeldy. The vegetable becomes part of the main cooking.

SADDLE OF LAMB ROLLED IN HERBS WITH TURNIPS AFTER FRANCES ATKINS

THE CRUST: Mix 1lb peeled and thinly sliced turnips, 1 sliced onion, ½ pint slightly soured cream, nutmeg, salt and pepper and cook at gas 6, 400°F (200°C) for 45 minutes. The cream must be infused into the turnip. Cool and refrigerate to set.

THE SAUCE: Take the bones from the saddle and make a stock with onions and carrots. Strain. Reduce and add sherry.

THE LAMB: Roll a boned eye of a saddle in a good handful of chopped, fresh garden herbs. Make a crust round the lamb with the turnip mixture. Hold together with a single layer of filo pastry. Glaze with a beaten egg yolk.

THE COOKING: Cook in a hot oven for 7–9 minutes. Take out and slice. Place on a dessertspoon of sauce made with the stock and sherry. Garnish with herb flowers.

THE SOUTH DOWN LAMB

The decline of the reputation of the South Down sheep coincided with the animals being taken off the downs and turned on to fields of turnips, a throwback to the farming of the middle ages. Gravetye Manor is a monument to English catering, the gardens designed by William Robinson, the house dating back to the Tudor times, and under the direction of Peter Herbert it has maintained a dining-room that has always been among the first flight of country house hotels after the war.

In early summer the saddle might be rolled plainly around asparagus spears, but later in the year the tougher, blander meat will take this robust mix, extravagant in the wines used, not to mention garlic. The red of the beetroots stains the sauce.

SADDLE OF LAMB WITH A BASIL STUFFING, SPINACH AND BEETROOT AFTER GRAVETYE MANOR

THE STOCK: Bone the saddle. Set the meat aside. Roast the bones in the oven with 1lb mirepoix of mixed vegetables until brown. Remove and put bones and mirepoix in a pan with 2 cloves of garlic, 6 fresh tomatoes, a sprig of thyme. Deglaze the roasting pan with ½ pint white wine. Pour over the bones. Add water to cover. Simmer 3 hours. Sieve. Cool.

THE STUFFING: Finely chop 6 shallots and a large clove of garlic. Sauté in 2 tablespoons warmed olive oil. Add 3oz butter. Mix in 12oz fresh white breadcrumbs and a good sprig or two of basil. Season with salt, pepper, tabasco and allow to cool.

THE BEETROOTS: Wash the baby beetroots. Plunge into boiling water for 5 minutes. Take out and peel off the skin. Put the beetroots in an empty pan with garlic, thyme and shallots. Add a glass of Hermitage. Reduce. Add a pint of the lamb stock, bring to the boil, cover with buttered paper and braise for an hour.

THE LAMB: Season the saddle well. Roll the stuffing around the outside of the meat. Lay out a good measure of pig's caul and wrap up the saddle and stuffing tightly. Leave in fridge for half an hour to settle.

THE COOKING: Heat a frying pan and seal the meat quickly. Put into a hot oven and roast for 8–10 minutes. Take out and leave to rest. Reduce the rest of the lamb stock by half. Add the beetroots and their cooking liquor. Reduce by one-third again. Finish with butter. Pick out the beetroots and keep warm with the lamb. Strain the sauce.

TO SERVE: Wash spinach. Place the wet leaves with a knob of butter in the pan with a little garlic and cook quickly for 30 seconds. Take out and press dry. Lay the spinach out on the plate. Slice the lamb and lay on the spinach with the beets. Surround with the sauce.

FRENCH LAMB

For the French kitchen, lamb, as opposed to mutton, was the prime meat. Best of all was the unweaned and ungrazed young lamb – the lamb of Pauillac – an idea that was, of course unthinkable to the peasant.

Joël Robuchon opens another page. Although at first sight it might seem unduly onerous, it translates easily into the home kitchen. More than half the work can be done well ahead. It has spawned variations, with different herbs accentuated, and repays cooking a few times to explore the options. The herbs and salt infuse the meat.

ROAST BEST END OF LAMB IN
A SALT CRUST WITH HERBS

THE STOCK: Bone and trim the best end. Put the bones in a deep, heavy pan to brown. Add chopped carrot, onion, celery, garlic. Deglaze. Cover with cold water. Skim. Simmer. Remove the bones and reduce to 60ml.

THE CRUST: Chop the leaves off 15 sprigs of thyme and 1 of rosemary. Mix with 300g salt, the whites of 2 eggs, 400g flour, and water and knead to a smooth dough. Let rest 15 minutes.

THE LAMB: Mix 2 tablespoons chopped parsley with 20g white breadcrumbs. Season the lamb, and roll in the crumb mix. Wrap in a sheet of reserved fat. Roll out half the crust, wrap the lamb up and seal. Brush with a glaze of egg yolks, sprinkle some more salt on to the outside of the parcel, and seal again with more egg wash.

THE COOKING: Roast in a very hot oven for 16 minutes for pink. Reduce the stock in a heavy pan. Add 4 leaves of basil. Add 200ml cream, or *crème fraîche*. Reduce. Add butter and thyme.

TO SERVE: Present the lamb in its crust at table. Break open. Take the lamb out of its barding and carve thinly. Serve the sauce separately. Garnish with egg noodles and carrots and courgettes sliced into lengths the same thicknesses as the noodles.

PORK: THE GENTLEMAN
WHO PAID THE RENT

PIGS ENJOYED A family relationship with people, shambling around medieval towns; left to roam in the forests around villages; kept at the bottom of the garden or the allotment. And the pig contributed a reassuring part of the cooking, too: roast pork with crackling and apple sauce for high days, sausages for low, fat for cooking. The pork pie, the ham sandwich, eggs and bacon were all ideas of the last century. In small communities the killing of a pig provided a Sunday activity. Everyone joined in and took away with them a section of meat, to last them, fresh and cured, through the coming weeks.

Somehow pigs always managed to fit in. They ate the whey from the cheese, manured the meadows for the corn, and were sold to bring in extra money at market days. The pig was the gentleman who paid the rent. Anyone who could afford one, or who had grazing rights, kept one. Pigs were a good investment, with as many as fourteen offspring at a good birth and needing only a minimum of looking after.

THE WILTSHIRE INDUSTRY

Wiltshire came to be seen as the centre of pig-breeding because of its great oak forests which dominated the Saxon landscape. And there was another reason: it was on the main drovers' road west to Bristol.

The cheese and bacon industry in Wiltshire began around Chippenham in the sixteenth century. The land had been cleared, was well-tilled and good for grazing. The important elements of the economy were all to do with livestock. In order, they were butter, beef, bacon, mutton and wool. On the northern fringe and to the south, the land was more open, the soil chalky. Here, the crops were cereal: barley, wheat, lamb, malt and wool. The agriculture split between chalk and cheese, hence the saying.

Wiltshire bacon and sausages were made famous by one family. John Harris was a butcher in Calne. His widow and sons John and Henry, carried on the business after he died in 1791, but it was still a good week if they killed five or six pigs and had sold out by Saturday night. After their mother died, both brothers opened shops but carried on curing bacon in the back. Before the railways, the drovers came through Calne with herds of Irish pigs destined for London. The reputation of the Harris's bacons spread, not only with the drovers, but also with fashionable society bound from London to Bath and back. But in 1847 the potato famine wiped out the pig trade with Ireland. John Harris sent his son George to America to see what was happening in the new world. He saw ice coolers for the first time.

MODERN BACON

Pigs were always killed in winter. The cures were tough, hard mixes to ensure the meat would last. George Harris saw that, with ice, he could change that.

He built an ice house with charcoal walls and an iron floor. The ice was collected locally, in winter, at first, and later imported from Norway. The ice house meant not only that the pigs could be cured all year, but that a far milder cure could be used. Only seven years after opening their ice house, in 1856 the demand for Harris bacon was so great that the family built a railway between Calne and Chippenham. The patent on the charcoal-insulated house had secured the future of the business. By 1885, they were taking pigs from twenty-five counties and exporting to America. Between 2,000 and 3,000 pigs were killed a week, and a mile-and-half of sausages were made a day. The Harris family finally gave up their interest in the company in 1920 and took over another company, which was to become almost as well-known, Bowyer.

At the height of the trade, within a ten-mile radius there were ten other curers at work, each with their own style and slightly different recipe. These early hams, especially the air-dried ones, can be found occasionally – Sandridge Farm in Bromham has recently gone back to curing in the old way, and in Waberthwaite in Cumbria, the Woodall family cure and air-dry – but, like the York ham, these almost forgotten articles, although the equivalents of Bayonne and Parma, have carelessly been allowed to die out.

THE OLD BREEDS

Native pigs were boar-like and straight-faced. Up to the middle of the eighteenth century, there were two main breeds: a small, dark animal with prick ears in the north; a paler, larger, lop-eared barrelesque beast to the south. They foraged in the woodlands and were only domesticated as the woods were cleared and the enclosures established.

New blood came from China, in the form of dish-faced animals. English breeders were enthusiastic about these new strains, as the pigs were promiscuous. The early products of these matings were given rolling, echoing names: Essex Saddleback, Landrace, Large White, Tamworth, Lincolnshire Curly Coat, Gloucester Old Spot, Long White Lop, Old Glamorgan, Oxford Sandy, Yorkshire Blue, Dorset Gold Tip, Large Black. Often as not the pigs lived off the waste from the breweries, which explains the couplings with pub and beer names.

THE PORK PIE

At the same time that Calne was starting in bacon, Melton Mowbray was developing the pork pie. Again, it was the pigs around a cottage cheese industry, this time Stilton, that were used, and again its popularity spread because it was a lasting, portable food on the coach road to London. And just as Bath had made Wiltshire cures fashionable, this time it was the hunt which blessed the pie industry.

The traditional hot water paste was raised by hand on a wooden, bell-shaped mould, but fell out of use when it began to clog up the new machines. The stock in English cookery is found here, reduced to a jelly, and used to set the inside of the pie. Only the meaty filling was eaten. The pastry was often thrown away.

PORK PIE AFTER YE OLDE PORKE PIE SHOPPE AT MELTON MOWBRAY

THE PASTRY: Melt lard in boiling water. Add flour and salt. Work to a dough and roll into ball. Using a mould, work the pastry up the sides using both hands and squeezing with the little finger.

THE PIE: Mince pork. Season with salt and pepper. Place in the pie mould. Cover with a pastry lid. Prick the top to let out the steam. Bake. Make a stock of the bones and trotters. Pour this in after the baking.

Being so much a part of the community perhaps mitigated against the pig becoming too much of a restaurant or tavern food. Fresh pork has played a much lesser part in the cooking of north Europe. The kitchen has often been content to hand over big areas of skill and expertise to the butcher. Pork butchery is a relatively extended process, compared to that of other meats. Even Escoffier focused more on the use of hams than other cuts and meats. But he gives one recipe for a pork pie.

HOT PORK PIE AFTER ESCOFFIER

Line the inside of a pie dish with thin slices of ham. Season some fresh pork well with salt, pepper, sage, and mushrooms. Put a layer of small, thick slices of fresh pork across the bottom, then a layer of potato, then chopped onion, more pork, more potato and finishing on top with pork. The ratio should be 3 parts pork to 3 parts potato to 1 part onion. Add water. Cover with a short paste or puff pastry trimmings. Brush with a beaten egg. Bake 2 hours.

LESSONS FROM CHINA

The limited repertoire with which European cooks were content for pork is exposed by other cuisines. In parts of China, pork provides the most authoritative statement about the cooking. Many of the 300-plus dishes found on menus in Cantonese restaurants rely on pork, where beef and lamb are almost peripheral. Dim-sum is made up almost exclusively of pork dishes. The much bastardized cliché of sweet-and-sour pork remains a crystallization of an idea of Chinese cooking.

The difference is not just agricultural but also technological. The ovens for roast pork, suckling pig, or spare ribs in Chinese cooking are tall, cylindrical rockets with open flames in the centre coming up from the floor, and space on either side so the fats can drip away. They are tall enough to hang a whole pig. In English cooking, roast pork was a seasonal dish, another mark that autumn was the high time of English cooking, hence the apple sauce. But the culinary differences are yet more decisive. In Cantonese cooking, the ribs of the suckling pig are liberally smeared with a seasoning of salt, sugar and five-spice and then left to hang, so that the flesh is part-cured. The skin is pricked and washed with vinegar. It is basted with boiling water to tighten. In the cooking, it is basted with oil. With *char sui* the neck, properly half fat and half meat, is macerated in a sweet-and-sour mix of hoisin, sesame, oyster sauces; then hung to dry before cooking.

Another example of the lengths the Chinese have stretched the cooking of pork, is found in this recipe for white cooked pork, sometimes found in Szechuan restaurants.

WHITE CUT PORK

THE MEAT: Simmer a lean or thick end of belly pork in water for an hour. Take out the pork and rinse under cold water to firm up the flesh. Refrigerate overnight.

THE SAUCE: Mix chopped garlic, spring onions, red chilli with 3 parts thick soy sauce to 1 part sesame oil, 1 part rice wine, 1 part chilli oil and 1 teaspoon sugar.

TO SERVE: Slice the pork as thinly as possible and arrange around the plate. Pour the sauce into the centre.

SEASONINGS

Where there is agreement in the cooking, is in the resilience and fire of the seasonings. Pork stands up to the sharper, acidulated seasonings, its blandness a platform from which shots of seasoning can be launched. Where lamb looks to the mellower, gentle flavours of fruits and herbs, and where beef can equal the single-mindedness of strong flavours; pork has a sympathy with the tart stridency of lemons, vinegars or more subtle variations, like gherkins or juniper berries.

PORK WITH GHERKINS AND MUSTARD

Fry the pork chop or tenderloin in butter. Mix separately mustard, chopped gherkin, a drop of vinegar and cream. Drain the fat from the pan and deglaze with the sauce.

Sheila Hall was a finalist in the Best British Meat Dishes contest, run by the *Sunday Times* in 1977 with this clever recipe which diligently goes to the lengths of making a pork stock rather than relying on the more common use of wine or cider.

PORK GENIÈVRE

THE STOCK: Chop the neck bones and add to cold water. Season with juniper berries, black peppercorns, parsley, garlic, onion, celery, salt. Cook 3 hours. Cool and skim off any fat.

THE MARINADE: Lay pork steaks in a marinade of 1 part olive oil, to 1 part lemon, to 3 parts gin, seasoned with crushed juniper berries and garlic. Leave 3 hours.

THE COOKING: Brown mushrooms and shallots in butter. Add the pork steaks. Brown either side. Pour on the marinade and the stock. Simmer for about 30 minutes depending on thickness. Take out the steaks. Add a little cream and season with lemon. Serve the steaks on croûtons with the sauce over and garnished with parsley.

The cream used to adjust the seasoning is unfashionable now, but more in the modern and the restaurant style is the deliberation of this salad developed by Leigh Stone-Herbert while he was cooking at his family country-house hotel, Gravetye Manor in Sussex. He uses a vinaigrette in place of cream. The exactness of the execution sets it out.

HAM AND LENTIL SALAD AFTER LEIGH
STONE-HERBERT

THE HAM: Braise the hock of ham in a rich stock. De-fat. Chill. Slice thinly. Dress with a thick emulsion of mustard, shallot, sunflower oil and vinegar.

THE LENTILS: Soak until the lentils have almost begun to germinate so that more of the starch has turned to sugar. Cook in chicken stock flavoured with star anise. Combine with the ham on a bed of curly endive and sliced tomatoes.

CHICKENS: CHILDREN OF TECHNOLOGY

THE COCKEREL, REMEMBER, was king of the farmyard, a symbol of independence and virility; the hen, an example of family life. Yet in barely more than a decade, they were herded indoors and separated from their children, their natural order inverted. Even the architecture of the great, long, low huts of the battery farms was that of the gulags.

THE LONG ROAD FROM INDIA

The forefathers of today's nameless inmates were the red jungle fowl, *gallus gallus*, of north India and the eastern peninsula, south towards Sumatra. Their dawn crowing was the voice of spiritual awakening. Their first encounters with humans may well have been for sacrifice in religious rituals, rather than food. Breeds like the pugnacious Asil were kept as fighting birds. Their spurs were taped, and contests were tests of stamina and went on for days.

By the fourteenth century BC the chicken had migrated along the trade routes west, far enough to appear on Egyptian seals. Early Britons kept fowls for pleasure and diversion, not for table.

Most of these early breeds were scrawny, shy birds perhaps not even worth the eating. By the middle ages, Chaucer describes lowly farms populated by cockerels and hens. They were by then a significant part of the diet, but few farmers understood about feeding patterns to breed on any significant commercial scale.

FROM FIGHTING, TO BREEDING

Fighting was a means of culling the weaker cocks, while there was still enough food outside. Cock-a-leekie soup was reputedly made with the losing bird in a fight, an idea supported by the extravagant use of what would have been the flush of leeks as the frosts set in.

COCK-A-LEEKIE SOUP (TRADITIONAL)

Take an equal weight of leeks to chicken. Wash and chop half the leeks, and lay in a pot. Lay the chicken on top. Cover with cold water. Bring to a simmer. Skim. Season. Cover, and cook slowly. Half-an-hour before the end of the cooking, chop the rest of the leeks and add to the pan.

Parliament finally banned cock fighting in 1849. But the sport turned, almost immediately, into a less cruel form of exhibitionism: the poultry show. America imported chickens from southern Europe and Asia to create new show birds which filled even Madison Square Garden. Some of these, like the Blue Andalusian, could hardly lay enough eggs to survive, so poorly had their breeding developed. By the turn of the century, commercial pressures had taken over and the aims of the fancier and the business owners divided. In America, between 1930 and 1950, nearly all the established breeds had been replaced with birds that would thrive indoors, and produce high meat ratios and good numbers of eggs. This was what the supermarkets wanted, and the more powerful they became, the more the industry responded.

The same happened swiftly in England. Urbanization, and the first world war, had already opened the door to factory production. The small farms that supplied London and which gave their names to the breeds – the Dorking (which figures in Roman chronicles of the first century BC), Orpington, Ixworth, Sussex – went for property development to satisfy the expansion of London. Some of these cottage industries had been quite sophisticated. Capons for banquets were force-fed on skimmed milk, like geese for foie gras. The whiteness of the flesh was prized. By 1950, major British birds of 100 years before, including the Spanish and the Cochin Chinas, had been replaced. After 400 years colonizing and annexing new worlds, the British imperialistic streak embarked on a period of introspection, and turned on its own livestock and countryside.

INSIDE THE HUTS

Poultry are sensitive to light. Under bright lights birds become frisky, aggressive, even hysterical. If the light is turned down, the birds are calmed. Hens lay only in daylight. The family has a strict social code, that runs right across large groups. Hens are faithful to the one male. The stronger birds will eat most of the feed. But in groups bigger than 100, the birds cannot cope. They become disorientated, and their natural pecking order breaks down.

The eggs for hatching are taken from the hen, and laid out on trays for three to five days, fumigated, and then placed in ovens at 99°F for eighteen days. They are turned and shifted every hour. The chick lives on the protein of the yolk, and can survive up to seventy-two hours after cutting its way out of the shell.

The white of a freshly laid egg holds the yolk tightly in the centre. As the elasticity in the albumen weakens, the yolk moves closer to the shell. An old test for a fresh egg was to put it in a salt solution. The egg should sink. Once older than four days, it rises. Most eggs today will not have left the central packing stations before they have gone beyond the point the classical kitchen would have termed 'fresh'.

THE COCKEREL'S FATE

The supermarket also demanded smaller birds to fit the needs of the nuclear family. Today, these are killed at about seventy days, but before the batteries a bird was allowed to grow to a weight of 7lb and more. Identities have been lost in scientific codings and commercial secrecy. So too the sex, because it was the cockerel who went to make the finest dishes, not the hen, who would have been kept for her eggs. A *coq au vin* is what it says, and is hard to achieve with a modern chicken. Recipes demand the blood and suggest a link to cock fighting, as with cock-a-leekie. The marination might well have been to counter the toughness of a pugnacious older champion, who had had his last fight. Cooking the onions and mushrooms separately is an effective idea. The proper wine to drink is the same as that used in the cooking.

COQ AU VIN (TRADITIONAL)

THE BLOOD: Beat with 2 tablespoons of wine and keep in the fridge.

THE MARINADE: To a bottle of red wine (NB: most recipes use red wine, but in areas where white predominates, Riesling and Chardonnay are used, but without the blood), add 2 tablespoons oil, thyme, bay, parsley and coarsely ground pepper. Cut the cockerel into 8 and lay in the marinade overnight.

THE COOKING: Wipe the chicken pieces dry. Sauté in a casserole with butter and strips of bacon or belly pork. Flambé with a little cognac. Add flour. Brown the meat well on all sides without burning. Pour over the marinade. Season with garlic, salt and pepper. Cover, and simmer for about an hour.

THE VEGETABLES: In a second pan, brown some small whole onions in butter. After 10 minutes, add sugar. Shake regularly, so they do not burn. In a third pan, stew some mushrooms in butter for 5 minutes. Add both of these to the chicken. Cook on for 15 minutes.

TO SERVE: Take out the pieces of chicken, onions and mushrooms. Take some of the cooking liquid, whip in the blood away from the heat, and pour over the chicken.

INTO THE POT

The chicken was, and is, central to French cooking, just as the pig is to the Cantonese and pasta to the Italians. Come the revolution, the influx of people from the provinces to Paris brought dishes like egg mayonnaise or *omelettes fines herbes* into the currency of the Parisian bistro. So too the *coq au vin*, and the *poule au pot*, and a range of country dishes from each department.

The new delegates doubtless wanted to eat their own cooking, but more than that, there was a certain flamboyant patriotism in bringing all the foods and all the styles of cooking together in the capital, as a focus of the variety and richness of the culture whose future was being decided. The cockerel was the symbol of farmyard France.

Escoffier gave more than 230 recipes for chicken. He classed the supremes of queen and spring chicken as among the finest entrées. These were persuasive vehicles for his sequences of sauces, garnishes and, in whole roasts, stuffings.

From English cooking he borrowed only chicken grilled on a spit, stuffed in a pie, and poached whole with vegetables, the stock going to make a béchamel to coat the serving. This seems an aberration. A chicken in a pot was the gastronomic crystallization of the French idea. English pies and roasts with bacon, sausages, bread sauce and perhaps even a stuffing of crumbs, lemon rind, parsley and thyme, are essentially dry dishes, where the French were pre-occupied with variations of wet cookings: in wine, in stocks, in whatever. The pot was part of the culture. The recipes moved with the seasons.

SUMMER CHICKEN
IN A POT WITH 40 GARLIC CLOVES

Salt and pepper the inside of a chicken. In a pot, place 40 unpeeled garlic cloves, a cup of fruity virgin olive oil and a good bouquet of fresh chopped herbs. Turn the chicken in this aromatic liquid so it is well-coated. Stand the chicken on the garlic cloves. Cover the pot, and seal up with flour and water paste so no air can get out. Bake in a low oven for 1½ hours.

TO SERVE: Break open the casserole at the table to release the spectacular perfumed steam. Serve with toasted bread, on to which the softened garlic can be spread.

AUTUMN CHICKEN IN A POT WITH
ROOT VEGETABLES

Place the whole chicken in the pot. Cut thickly leeks, parsnip, carrot, swede or other root vegetable. Arrange the vegetables around the bird. Season with garlic. Put on a heavy cover, or seal with tin foil. Bake for 1½ hours.

THE BIRDS FROM BRESSE

For the Lyons dynasty, there was only one chicken. The Bresse chicken is active, graceful, black-eyed. It has bright red combs, face and wattles; snow-white ear lobes; blue-grey legs and feet; the plumage black, with a brilliant beetle-green sheen. If white, it is a pure white, blue-white beak; red or sooty face; ear lobes blue-white; legs and feet blue, from which they take their nickname, *les pattes bleues*.

The Bresse chicken retains its identity through careful husbandry. Since 1936, the area in which chickens can be bred and still be called Bresse chicken has been marked out.

The ground has a rich fauna of varied grasses, insects and small animals. The soil is high in calcium, which strengthens the birds' bones. In 1957 a further protection was brought in, by labelling the birds for sale under the tag of an *appellation d'origine*. Since 1970, intensive factory farming in the area has been discouraged. In all, the protected area is a rectangle 100 kilometres from north to south, 40 kilometres east to west. The birds are raised on natural cereals and dairy products. They range freely and are allowed to live from four to five months.

The flesh is silken and game-like. Commercially, the economics are the reverse of the battery hangars: the flesh-to-bone ratio is poor, compared to a battery-reared bird. Even a fair-sized hen will only feed two. But on the other hand, it commands twice the price.

Point was from Louhans, the capital of the Bresse region. He gave this evolved variation on a *poule au pot* the name of his restaurant.

VOLAILLE PYRAMIDE AFTER FERNAND POINT

THE CHICKEN: Sweat a diced carrot and a diced leek in butter in a casserole. Add the chicken and brown all over. Add enough veal stock to half-cover the bird. Add a glass or 2 of white wine. Season. Cover. Braise slowly, basting the top of the bird regularly.

THE SAUCE: Make a roux with flour, butter and the stock from the chicken. Add onion, clove, carrot. Cook out the flour. Add butter. Liaise with 2–3 egg yolks. Season.

Where many restaurants have given up on chicken in favour of other birds, Paul Bocuse has maintained his link with his past. His menus continue to find room for Bresse birds: poached with salt, celery, leeks, turnips, carrots, horn of plenty mushrooms; or boned and stuffed chicken named after Joanne Nandron, the layer between skin and flesh filled with truffle, the stuffing made with veal fillet, double cream, carrots, turnips, celeriac, peas and beans, the whole re-formed and wrapped inside a pig's bladder and cooked in white chicken stock.

INSIDE A PIG'S BLADDER

Cooking a chicken inside a pig's bladder is a Lyonnais tradition. You need a small chicken, for a start. A fresh pig's bladder is not much bigger than the kind of bandage you put over a cut thumb. A frozen one will not do, because it loses its elasticity. Carefully, insert two fingers inside, clench them, and the bladder can be drawn over the hand. The bladder grabs the hand and seals it tightly, which is the purpose of the cooking. But it is still a fragile membrane, and can be expanded slowly and carefully, using water from a hot tap to balloon out. Once it is a reasonable size (and not all pigs have bladders of a reasonable size), the bird can be slipped inside and the ends tied tightly to seal it hermetically.

In practice, the modern kitchen buys ready-blown bladders that have been commercially dried and expanded to two feet long. All they need is soaking in water and vinegar for an hour, and then thorough washing. If the poaching liquid gets too hot, however, the bladder snaps and all is lost. Cooking *sous vide* does the job just as effectively, and is less delicate.

Christian Delteil at L'Arlequin in Battersea has revived the tactic. He soaks a chicken overnight in milk and water to blanch, then dries and seasons it. He makes a stuffing of chicken livers, pork, shallot minced and mixed with an egg, parsley and cream and crams the inside of the bird full, then slips it into the bladder, cutting the opening if necessary to get it in. He wets it with a little port or cognac and chicken stock and then seals up the end – a job for two – tightly wrapping it up with string, then brings it to a slow boil for an hour. The point is to flavour the bird from the inside, so it cooks in its own juices.

Similar strategies are found with the bird encased in the whole of a pig's stomach, or, borrowing from the south west, encased in salt.

WITH TRUFFLES . . .

Truffles were for a long time the other mark of Lyonnais cooking, and often served *en vessie*. This dish is credited to La Mère Brazier. The process seems sensitively geared to the small bistro. The short cooking time took account both of the small size of the bird and also the erratic timing of customers.

POULARDE POCHÉE DEMI-DEUIL

Make a good courtbouillon of leeks, carrots, turnips, celery, thyme, bay and smoked belly of pork. Cook for 1 hour and leave to cool. Stuff the inside of the skin of a Bresse chicken with slices of truffle. Poach the chicken in the courtbouillon for 15 minutes from when it starts to boil. Pull over to the side of the stove, and keep warm.

TO SERVE: Take out the vegetables and stew in butter. Strain the courtbouillon and reduce to 4 tablespoons. Using a wire whisk, beat in butter in small pieces to make a *beurre blanc* and pour this over the vegetables. Carve the chicken, and serve with a béarnaise spiked with horseradish.

There is no real point to doing this dish without prime truffles. The shavings and trimmings sold in cans are a waste of money. Just as with garlic, truffles need to be used deliberately and generously, or not at all. The tiny specks of black that riddled *nouvelle cuisine*, far from giving a frisson of excitement were, for the most part, facetious pretension. The chef may well have enjoyed opening the truffle box to get the full scent of what might now cost more than £100, but in the dining-room they are lost in small measure.

. . . AND CREAM . . .

Georges Blanc keeps this famous dish on the menu at his restaurant in Vonnas, previously La Mère Blanc. He points out that if the bird is a Bresse chicken of high quality, the cooking does not need a consommé. The chicken itself and the sugars brought out from the braising give all the taste to the sauce.

POULET À LA CRÈME COMME EN BRESSE
AFTER GEORGES BLANC

Flame and gut the chicken. Cut the bird up into pieces with a large knife. First remove the thighs, separating them in 2 (legs and upper thigh). Lift off the wings, and cut off the tips. Take off the breasts and cut across. Chop the carcass, the neck and keep the wing tips.

Take a large casserole, put it on a strong fire with a good measure of butter, and lay in the chicken pieces, adding salt and pepper. Let the chicken colour lightly all over.

Add 1 onion spiked with a clove, a clove of flattened garlic, a sprig of thyme and ½ bay leaf and the bones. Add more butter and 2–3 tablespoons of flour. Let the flour colour and cook through for an instant, wet with water so that all the ingredients are well covered. Mix, and allow to boil to effect the liaison. Cover and cook on a more moderate fire for around 30 minutes, depending on the size of the chicken.

At the end of the cooking, lift the chicken pieces out with a fork and put them in a second pot. Strain the rest of the sauce over the chicken through a muslin. Mix ½ litre of double cream with 3 egg yolks and add to the chicken. Do not allow the pan to boil after the cream has been added.

If necessary, adjust the consistency of the sauce with more cream or water. Check the seasoning and add a final squeeze of lemon. Serve on a large hot plate with a garnish of rice.

. . . AND VINEGAR

Blanc's chicken bears the same stamp as Point's, as if they were using the same score. A more marked evolution is visible in these two recipes for pan fried chicken with vinegar, one from Restaurant Nandron in Lyons in the early Fifties, the other from Michel Guérard at Eugénie-les-Bains in the early Seventies.

CHICKEN WITH TARRAGON VINEGAR
AFTER GIRARD NANDRON

Cut a chicken into pieces and brown in butter in a heavy pan. When well-coloured, deglaze with 2 tablespoons of tarragon vinegar, stirring with a wooden spoon. Add 2 peeled, seeded and crushed tomatoes. Cook slowly for 20 minutes. Take out the chicken. Sieve the pan juices. Season. Add a good measure of butter, and pour over the chicken pieces. Serve with soft bread fried in butter.

VINEGAR CHICKEN AFTER MICHEL GUÉRARD

THE CHICKEN: Cut up the chicken and brown in butter 5 minutes per side. Add 6 unpeeled cloves of garlic. Cook the breasts 20 minutes and the legs another 5. Pour off the fat. Add 5 tablespoons wine vinegar to deglaze. Half-cover the casserole and reduce at a fast boil so the vinegar perfumes the chicken. Take out the chicken and keep warm.

THE SAUCE: Mix white wine, Armagnac, mustard, tomato purée, pour into the pan and reduce at a boil, stirring all the time. Whisk in some cream, then take off the heat and build up a *beurre blanc* for a liaison. Strain the sauce, pressing the garlic cloves through the sieve to extract the last drops. Garnish with tomato concasse and chervil.

The classical kitchen made great use of the liquids which began life in the pot with a chicken. But a 'chicken' stock contained just as much veal, and was made from a basic white stock – mostly veal, with a little chicken and aromatics, cooked for three hours – to which were added carcasses, giblets and boiling fowls to bring it up to about half chicken, half veal. Modern variations are purer. The stock was not only the base for many of the 180 variations on consommé listed in the *Guide Culinaire*, but also provided a liquid for pale sauces, like a blanquette for veal, and was often used to cook vegetables.

In the modern kitchen, chicken stock has come to be used as a means of making the cooking lighter, an alternative to the heavy meat fonds or béchamels, and flexible enough to be used with fish.

The line between a stock and soup is thin, and more so with chicken than with other meats and fish. Nick Gill served this consommé, flavoured with smoke and herbs, as a starter at the country house hotel Hambleton Hall in Leicestershire.

SMOKED CHICKEN AND BASIL CONSOMMÉ
AFTER NICK GILL

Clarify a strong chicken stock by beating in a mix of egg whites and diced vegetables. Cook until the impurities have massed in the albumen of the egg white, and formed a good crust on the surface. Strain off the clear liquid underneath. Add basil and shards of smoked chicken. Allow to infuse in the broth and serve.

Other influences from far afield carry on the Victorian heritage of combining and adapting new produce as it reaches the markets, often from the other side of the globe. Philip Harris is English, but fell in love with Thailand and, since his return, has opened two Thai restaurants in London, both called the Bahn Thai.

CHICKEN AND GALANGAL SOUP AFTER
PHILIP HARRIS

Grate the flesh of a coconut. Add 2 tablespoons boiling water. Mix well and squeeze the liquid out over a sieve and bowl. Bring to a simmer, stirring all the time and then add ½ pint chicken stock. ('It is important not to allow the coconut to boil too hard, or it will separate and leave you with a layer of oil.') Add the juice of 1 lemon; shards of 2 kaffir lime leaves; a 2-inch stick of lemon grass, crushed and diced; and 5–10 slices of galangal (Laos Root) – about 4 teaspoons. Simmer for 2 minutes to draw out the flavour of the spices, then add 6oz sliced chicken breast. Simmer for 2–3 minutes to cook the chicken through. Season with fish sauce and pepper. Garnish with sliced red and green chillies and coriander leaves. 'It is delicious if eaten simply poured spoon by spoon over steamed rice.'

AWAY FROM LYONS

In other styles of cooking, like Cantonese, priorities turn around. Soya chicken deceives the eye, but is essentially chicken cooked in a pot, often with just water, not even stock. But for the final minutes the bird is plunged into a boiling, molasses-coloured solution of thick soy sauce and sugar, and left to infuse off the heat. The skin turns a roasted brown colour so it looks like a duck, and the flesh is indelibly permeated and has a salty casing on its outer perimeters. The marinade has been ushered from the front of the cooking, right to the end.

Away from the Lyonnais domination, the cooking takes on a different hue. This recipe is in fact Chinese, but it seems to embody the spirit of the modern kitchen as much as any other in this book, bringing together deliberate contrasts of texture, colour and flavour. It comes from the Mandarin Hotel in Hong Kong, which stares down over the Star ferry, a bizarrely opulent frontier post on the borders of east and west, a monument to air-conditioning and ease, in a city of fast moving and speculation; an institution where everything else seems transient. It has a number of fine kitchens, as it must in the most competitive restaurant city in the world.

CRISPY FRIED CHICKEN WITH FRIED SCALLOPS
AND HONEY-GLAZED HAM

THE CHICKEN: Mix white vinegar, honey, red vinegar, lemon juice in a pan, and boil. Set aside. Wash the chicken, smear inside with salt. Brush the outside with the vinegar solution. Hang for 3 hours.

THE COOKING: Heat the wok with oil until boiling, reduce the heat, add the chicken and fry whole for 20 minutes. Remove the chicken. Chop. Debone and arrange to the right of an oval plate.

THE HAM: Marinate Yunnan ham (similar to Parma) with honey. Cover with cornstarch, and boil for 2 minutes. Slice thinly.

THE SCALLOPS: Cut in half twice as many scallops as you have ham slices. Smear with cornstarch and fry in boiling oil for 2 minutes. Arrange scallops and ham on the left side of the plate, and garnish with sweet fried walnuts.

GEESE: GUARDIANS OF THE FARMYARD

OTHER BIRDS HAVE found similar standing to chickens at different points in history. The goose was an important part of the economy of the middle ages. The quills went for pens and arrow flights, the feathers for pillows, the fats for cooking and embrocation. They were the guardians of the farmyard, admired for their unflappable and placid courage. Their image as rather dull and stupid seems to have come much later, perhaps an urban prejudice. Ancient Britons appear to have kept them, like chickens, as pets and probably did not eat them at all.

Until Norman times there were enough wild geese to be easily shot or trapped, but at about that time, for reasons that are not clear, the numbers dropped. One reason could have been that drainage and cultivation of the coastal areas frightened the birds off, or made the marshlands inhospitable. In Norfolk and Lincolnshire, where large tracts of the fens were only partially reclaimed, the first attempts at domestic breeding began and lasted to the nineteenth century. In the breeding season, the birds were kept in triple rows of wicker pens, one stacked on top of the other. Food was laid out nearby for the ganders, and twice a day the goose herd walked the gaggle to water. Once the eggs were hatched the young goslings would follow their parents to the fens, where they looked after themselves for the summer. Plucking was done five times a year. The first time, on Ladyday, for quills; the other times, at Midsummer, Lammas, Michaelmas and Martinmas, for feathers only.

FLIGHTS OF FEATHERS

When Henry V demanded more than a million feathers for his archers to use in his French expedition, the counties supplied: Surrey, Nottingham, Sussex and Derbyshire, 15,000 each; Worcestershire, Berkshire, Warwickshire, Leicestershire, Rutland, Staffordshire, Northumberland, and Yorkshire, 30,000 apiece; Gloucestershire, Bedfordshire, Southampton and Buckinghamshire, 40,000 each; Somerset, Cambridgeshire, Dorset, Huntingdonshire, Hertfordshire, Essex, Suffolk and Norfolk, 50,000 each; Kent and Lancashire, 100,000 each. Roughly speaking, there must have been more than a quarter of a million geese in captivity at the time.

Michaelmas was the seasonal day set aside for eating goose, roasted with a side sauce of stewed apples and perhaps a sage and onion stuffing. There was a force of logic behind this: the geese had been fattened on the cleared stubble after the harvest, scallion onions would have needed to be eaten up, while the first of the windfall apples would have been on the ground. Rabbits, too, might have formed part of the dish, either the legs cooked inside the goose as something less rich for the children to eat; or roasted under the goose and basted in the fat.

In East Anglia, the local dish in spring was green goose, or goslings. They were stuffed with butter and seasoned. 'Then place the goose in a well greased tin down in the hearth before a steady clear fire and turn alternate sides to the warmth from time to time,' Judith Montrose wrote in the *Daily Chronicle*, in April 1922. The sauce in hotels in the area was tomato or gooseberry, but the local sauce was sorrel. The leaves were stewed in butter, strained, and seasoned with a thick cream and teaspoon of sugar.

FEAST DAYS

Often quoted from different sources, either as a Stafford pie or Yorkshire pie, was the goose as the outside wrapping of a pie of different poultry. Some sources give the date as 1790, though it could surely be earlier. The gross use of both turkey and duck, neither of which might have been that common, suggest it comes from a feudal banquet, although it was also a village feast in the West Riding. The goose and the duck go on the outside, so the fats seeps through to the centre. The trick is to use an 'amazing quantity of butter and flour'. It gives an idea of the different sizes of birds 200 years ago.

YORKSHIRE OR STAFFORD GOOSE PIE

Bone a large fat goose, a turkey, a duck, a fowl. Make a forcemeat of woodcocks, hare and tongue (optional). Season each generously with salt, pepper, mace and allspice. Wrap the forcemeat in the hen, and then the hen in the duck, the duck in the turkey, and the turkey in the goose, seasoning each layer well. 'The crust should have a Flower or Knob by which to lift it, as it must not be cut, but kept to cover the pie.'

THE GUILD OF ROASTERS

The classical kitchen disliked the flesh of the goose. Escoffier said: 'It is really only used in ordinary household and bourgeois cookery.' There is an element of over-familiarity in this dismissal.

For centuries, the guild of roasters in Paris cooked little else, so much so that they came to be known as *oyers* and described themselves as such in their articles. Escoffier might well have wanted to distance his kitchen from such street craft. The exception is, of course the liver, of which more later. But, in a real sense, the goose did not enter the repertoire of either the classical or the modern kitchens.

QUAIL: AN APPROACHING STORM

E SCOFFIER WAS MORE persuaded to the merits of smaller birds like quail, which one suspects as being a generic name for a great many small birds. He almost enthuses: 'Other than spit roasting, which is to be preferred to oven roasting, quails admit to two other excellent methods of cooking: they may be cooked in a casserole with butter, or poached in a good, well-flavoured, gelatinous veal stock.'

Just as the goose populated the marshlands and was often seen in dense white flocks in early Europe, or else in militaristic flying patterns along its migratory routes; so quail was a feature of the evening horizon. They massed in great flocks, sometimes so vast and tightly packed that the sky would darken. From a distance, they looked like thunder arriving at a ferocious speed. The *Daily Mail* of 1926 recorded an incident from a century before, where a shooter in Lincolnshire bagged sixteen birds with a single shot.

Such massing is given as one explanation of the Miracle of Santa Lucia in Sicily. The island was starving and besieged, when suddenly a flock of birds, exhausted from their long flight, fell helpless to the ground, to be gathered by the grateful people.

A plausible explanation of this fanciful story is that although quails fly long distances, they do not have any great stamina, and tend to travel in short hops. If they hit a strong, adverse wind, they could quickly become exhausted and drop, literally, out of the sky. At other times, they have been taken to be the manna from heaven, although *Exodus* suggests that the manna was there on the ground in the morning, while quails would have been unlikely to have flown at night.

IN AND OUT OF FASHION

Either way, in the Twenties quails were quite the thing. A London club abandoned the cooking altogether, and issued members with spirit lamps, rations of vine leaves, bacon and seasoned birds, and let each table do the cooking itself. Although the great flocks no longer appear over northern Europe, earlier this century at the beginning of September and again in March, as many as three million were caught as they passed over Egypt, netted in great 100-yard wide meshes held aloft on tall poles, or lured to the ground by grain laid out over pit traps. The birds were packed alive, 100 to the tray, the tray covered with a taut linen gauze to protect their heads, and transported 50,000 to a ship.

With potatoes, they were the return cargo for boats bringing Fords and Chevrolets via Marseilles. Passengers spoke of the eerie sound of the rustling of thousands of tiny feet below deck. In 1937, the cruelty led to Parliament stopping the trade, which has revived only now on a small scale in the UK, using imported Japanese stock.

But in the middle ages poulterers stocked quail, and they seem to have been plentiful. Recipes from the fifteenth century suggested roasting, and seasoning with aniseed, ginger and cinnamon. A cold pie was baked with nutmeg, clove, pepper and sealed with butter.

The petiteness of quails appealed to the classical kitchen. Escoffier experimented with different casings in which they could nest: on an artichoke heart with chestnut purée for decoration; inside a hollowed-out Cox's orange pippin with a sauce of calvados; cold inside tangerine peel, with the breasts placed on a quail mousse.

Most flamboyant of all, the quail breast was diced with truffle trimming and brandy, fashioned into balls, poached inside a muslin cloth in stock and then dropped into hollowed-out truffles poached in champagne; the whole sauced with demi-glace flavoured with quail fumet.

QUAILS IN CINDERS (TRADITIONAL)

Stuff the quail with forcemeat. Wrap first in a buttered vine leaf, then in a layer of salt pork fat, and then in two sheets of strong buttered paper. Place on the hearthstone of the fire and cover with very hot cinders for 30 minutes, replacing the cinders with hot ones at intervals. Remove the outer scorched paper and serve.

CASSEROLE OF QUAIL AFTER ESCOFFIER

Put the quail in a casserole with butter. Cover. Bake. Take out and put in a hot terrine with 8–10 peeled and seeded white grapes per bird. Deglaze the casserole with dry white wine, *verjus* (the juice of unripened grapes, used in place of vinegar in early cooking: substitute a good sharp vinegar) and ½ tablespoon of game fumet per bird. Pour over the quail.

SMOKED QUAIL WITH RED PEPPERS

Slice the red peppers. Heat some oil in a wok. Add a clove of diced garlic. Add the quail and the red pepper. Stir fry. Serve on a green salad.

DUCK: THE RISE TO RESPECTABILITY

IT WAS DUCK that eventually replaced chicken on restaurant menus. The classical kitchen had been strangely wary, as if ducks were too closely associated with the farmyard, or that the use of the dark meat was somehow too hedonistic.

Reservations remained until quite recently. The first push in the trade was for the livers. The breasts were sold separately, and the legs went to commercial pâtés, both essentially by-products, not main line meats.

Unusually, the classical kitchen singled out one breed as a focus of attention, the Rouen. These birds are slaughtered by strangling, and are not bled. The flesh is therefore much darker and they have to be eaten within twenty-four hours. The Rouen is unusual also, in that it is associated with the town of Yvetot, a dry area with hardly a spring or river in its circumference, suggesting that these birds were themselves imports. They are large, weighing up to 5½lb by four months, well-suited to spit roasting, not dissimilar to the now virtually extinct English Aylesbury, but almost twice the size of its latterday rival, the Nantes.

LA TOUR D'ARGENT

The best known of duck restaurants is La Tour d'Argent in Paris. The building stands squarely on a corner of what is now an expensive *arrondissement*, the fifth, overlooking the Seine and at an angle to Notre-Dame. The Tour claims to be the oldest eating place in Paris, dating back to 1582. Certainly there was an inn hereabouts, where the vegetable wagons and boatmen stopped on their way to the Paris markets.

It took its name from a stone tower re-inforcement, built by Charles V, that glinted in the sun, near an auberge run by a Bernardine convent. One of the early chefs was Rourteau. He imitated the court practice of using ivory forks, and Henri IV ordered meals from him, to be sent up to the palace at the Louvre. Courtiers returned the favour by visiting the Tour. It was Rourteau's skill and standing that persuaded Henri IV to license the guild of *cuisiniers*, on condition they took their meats from the roasting guilds. The risk of fire in medieval towns gave the roasters a protected place in the guild hierarchy.

The ground floors of the Tour d'Argent are now a museum. A table is still set out for a dinner in 1867, when Czar Alexander II was to eat a meal of fifteen dishes, including quail pâté, ortolans and *bombe glacée*, and drink Chambertin 1846.

With an appropriate sense of history, Escoffier had a hand in establishing the present dynasty. He recommended a young chef, André Terrail, then working at the Cavendish Hotel in London to take over. That was in 1890.

André's son Claude still presides over the now panoramic dining room on the sixth floor, arranged in that rather eccentric manner of Fifties postcards, with every table looking out on the view of floodlit rooftops, the loudspeaker chatter of the tourists' boats rising from the river below.

THE PRESS

A head chef, Frederick Burdel, created *canard au sang*. He looked anything but the chef, coming out to table to carve the ducks in suit and waistcoat, with the air of an amiable country doctor. From holding back a few drops of blood to thicken the sauce of a *coq au vin*, Frederick took the classical kitchen into the age of the machine. The duck-press is borrowed from canal-lock technology: a conical, snub-nosed guillotine, through which the three-quarters cooked carcass is passed and crushed. As the winders spin shut, the juices pour out of what looks like a municipal fountain spout. The outside is worked in ornamental silver.

The first duck *au sang* was served in 1880. Each one has been numbered since. The roll call approaches three-quarters of a million.

The ducks are from Challans in the Vendée. They grow to 7lb in nine weeks, on a diet of corn, soya, fruit pulp and molasses. They are roasted, brought to the table to be shown, scarred rugby balls, then whisked away for serving in two stages. One: the suit-grey breast is carved into a sauce of the pressed juices, duck consommé, port, pepper, brandy, finished with butter. The garnish is three *pommes soufflés*. Two: new knives and forks; the legs arrive on a green salad with a potato vinaigrette. They have been crisped under the grill.

GARNISHES AND FLAVOURS

Many of the birds offered to the classical kitchen would have been wild. The mallard was probably the seminal bird, and formed part of the same group as swans, herons and even peacocks, much in favour for the medieval feast. Duck was also part of the English repertoire of game cooking in clubs and taverns, being in season from August to March, but at its best only in November and December. Much was made of whether they were shoreline birds, or had fattened inland on the stubble of the grain fields.

The classical kitchen sent its ducks to pot braise. The fats, unless these were birds of a considerably different configuration from those we know now, as they might well have been if they had been wild, were left to gather at the bottom of the pan and form the base of the sauces. Escoffier even advised against skimming off any of the fat. Recipes dictate: fry in butter, braise in red wine.

Little wonder the kitchen reached for sharp, colourful garnishes to offset these sludgy juices. English apple sauce seems restrained against the dandyish repertoires attributed to the French: pineapple, olives, cherries, mint, horseradish, fruit vinegars; or the earthy reinforcers like *cèpes*, mushrooms, turnips, chestnuts, or the mealy strains of pea.

Duck with orange, before it became a factory unit standard, was a sauce of demi-glace and brown veal stock, tinged with the zest and rind of an orange. An English variation was simpler; segments of orange lain underneath a roasting wild duck for the last ten minutes of cooking; then punctured and a nugget of sugared butter inserted in each. Garnished with watercress, it was one of the more picturesque examples of early cooking. The marriage of tastes is discernibly different from the corruption since then to fattier, domestic ducks, crystallized oranges and sucrose sauces;

the opposite pole of the mallard's more instinctive affinity with grapefruit rather than orange. Such corruption seeped in as other roles for the duck fat – in cooking and housekeeping – were replaced by rival products. The cooking grew lazy, even obese.

ROASTING

The English roasted ducks, as they did most of their game. To be able to serve roast duck with green peas at Whitsuntide was a mark of being ahead of the yearly chores, for a well-organized family. The apple sauce would have been designed for the back end of the year, just as it was with pork. Orange was an urban expression.

As the birds grew fattier through commercial production, so roasting continued to be an effective technique. On the spits in the taverns and inns, the fat would have dripped away naturally. The tactic transfers into domestic cooking. The English way to roast a duck is to pour the fat from the tray religiously, every fifteen minutes, for as dry a roast as possible. Here, there is a tap on the shoulder from the other side of the world.

CHINESE DUCKS

Whether Peking duck was influenced by the British colonists or vice versa, or whether two separate cultures simply arrived at a similar conclusion is unclear. But there does seem to have been some cross-fertilization that must have begun with the export of ducks to Europe, and influenced kitchen and dining-room.

The dish was developed with special ducks and ovens and exported originally, according to some sources, in 1875.

As with the Tour d'Argent's duck *au sang*, the serving was in two stages: the crisped skin with the pancakes and hoisin sauce first, the meat then stir-fried with vegetables. Now, in most restaurants, it comes as one, single-minded meat course.

The duck is scalded to shrink the skin and make it shiny; brushed with a sweet marinade of diluted honey; hung for at least a day in a draught; roasted over a tray of water to compensate for the dryness. The oils and fats run into the unpricked skin and help crisp it and turn it a rust brown.

The Cantonese way of roasting ducks is different from that of Peking, but no less successful. At the New World, in London's Chinatown, one of the largest dim-sum houses outside of Hong Kong with three massive dining-rooms on three floors, capable of seating 600-plus, the ducks are

Pekin/Aylesbury crosses. They are dry-stuffed with four Chinese soup spoons of salt, sugar, monosodium glutamate and five-spice, and the cavity stitched closed so the juices are kept in. The duck is then dipped in boiling water to tighten the skin, and into a solution of white vinegar slaked with Fen Chien wine, red vinegar and honey. From there, it hangs in a draught of an open window for at least a day. On the morning of service, the ducks are wiped dry, then lowered on their hooks into the sides of the oven and left to hang-roast for about fifty minutes. The skin becomes caramelized and crisp, while the fats drip off to leave a dark, moist flesh.

BOILING

In regional European cooking ducks were sometimes boiled, a habit that has fallen out of use except in a few small Welsh restaurants, where the technique has been adopted as a national dish. The recipe is recorded by Lady Llanover, Augusta Hall, an English woman who lived in Wales and published a collection in 1867. She calls for the cooking to be done in a double. A bain-marie will do. The style reeks of cooking on a cauldron over a fire.

SALT DUCK AFTER LADY LLANOVER

THE MARINADE: Rub the duck all over with ¼lb sea salt. Leave in the salt in a cool place, and turn occasionally over 2–3 days.

THE COOKING: Wipe the duck clean. Put it in a dry pot. Add ½ pint water to 1lb duck. Put the pot inside a bigger pot with water, and simmer for about 2 hours. Serve with onion sauce.

The railways broke up the network of small farms around Aylesbury that owed their standing to being in walking and cart distance of London. Lately, the whole of the duck production for Britain has focused on a single company, Cherry Valley, on the Norfolk and Lincolnshire borders. The difference between breeds has become indistinct.

GRESSINGHAM DUCK

But in the last ten years in Cumbria, a new strain of duck has been brought on. The Gressingham was developed by Peter Dodds, who went not to the commercial crosses that provided the sperm bank of most duck production, but back to the mallard itself. He crossed this with a Pekin. The result is a thick-fleshed, meatier bird, with breasts fatter than steaks and a high ratio of flesh to bone. Coming from wild ducks, they have thin skins and are relatively unfatty.

Jean-Yves Morel, a Lyonnais, settled in Haslemere in Surrey. The village retains a pre-war, Austin-seven charm, and the restaurant up on the raised pavement is tucked under the beams and timbers of an old cottage. The menu remains resolutely French. Morel was among the first chefs to adopt the Gressingham, developing the classical idea of two services and allying it to the cliché of duck with orange.

GRESSINGHAM DUCK WITH KUMQUATS
AFTER JEAN-YVES MOREL

THE MARINADE: Bone the duck and put the legs and thighs in a marinade of red wine, shallot, juniper and orange for 2 days.

THE COOKING: Take out the legs and thighs. Wipe dry. Braise slowly with a little of the marinade, in a low oven for 2 hours.

THE BREASTS: Char-grill the breasts, 5 minutes either side. Serve with the thighs and legs, and a little braising liquor as sauce. Garnish with kumquats.

The inspiration for Francis Coulson's duck dish, also usually using Gressingham's, is more old-fashioned, definitely English. Yet it sets itself a modern agenda, looking to offset four components on the plate. Use two ducks for four people.

TWO DUCKLINGS WITH TWO SAUCES
AFTER FRANCIS COULSON

THE DUCKS: Take the legs off the ducks, and set aside. Season the rest of the ducks, and put them on a bed of chopped celery, carrots and leeks, with the chopped peel of an orange and a lemon. Wet with 8 fl oz chicken stock. Roast in a pre-heated oven at around gas 4, 350°F (180°C) for 75–80 minutes.

Bone the legs and purée the meat. Add 2 large egg whites and mix to a smooth paste. Scrape out, and chill in a separate dish for 15 minutes. Set the mix on a bowl of ice and beat in 4 fl oz double cream. Butter some small dariole moulds and fill with the mousse. Put in a baking tin filled with hot water. Cover with foil. Bake at gas 4 for 15 minutes, or until firm. Keep warm.

When the ducks are cooked, drizzle honey on the breasts and return to the oven for 5 minutes, taking care they do not burn. Take out. Leave to stand. Carve off the breasts, and keep the carcass back for stock.

THE FIRST SAUCE: Pour off the excess fat from the baking tray. Stir in 1 tablespoon flour and cook on the top of the stove, adding 4 fl oz of tawny port or red wine, and 8 fl oz chicken stock. Simmer and reduce by half. Season and strain. Stir in chopped fruit, if liked, and set aside.

THE SECOND SAUCE: Sauté ½ diced onion in 5 tablespoons butter until soft, not brown. Stir in ¾oz flour and cook on 3 minutes, without letting the mix colour. Take off the heat and add 4 fl oz white wine and 1¾ pints chicken stock. Return to the heat, and add 2oz peeled and crushed filbert nuts and 2 bay leaves. Simmer at a low heat for 15 minutes, strain. Season, add 8 fl oz cream and reduce, uncovered, if too thin.

TO SERVE: Serve the breast on a heated plate, masked with the first sauce. Unmould the mousses and serve with the second sauce. Serve with a green vegetable and, if liked, a mixed fruit compote.

REGIONAL UNDERWRITING

At Gers, in the south-west of France, Pierre Koffmann's grandmother raised mulard ducks, crosses between muscovies and ordinary ducks, for foie gras. She pan fried the livers, adding diced shallot and white wine, then pulling the pan to the side of the range to cook slowly for an hour. Three-quarters of the way through she would add some breadcrumbs to drink up fat and wine, and create a thick sauce.

Since he first opened Tante Claire in Chelsea in 1977, Koffmann has been happy to underwrite his menus with regional dishes such as pig's trotters, lentil salad, *gratin savoyard*, piperade, *jambon de Bayonne*, *escargots bourguignonne*, albeit ordered precisely into the careful conceptions of modern cooking. Even his lobster was cooked in the wine of the region, Madiran.

He works with the whole duck. They make up two – three, if you include the variations on foie gras – major dishes on the menu.

When the ducks arrive, they are filleted and the lesser parts and giblets consigned to a *confit*. They are put into salt for twenty-four hours, washed, and then braised gently without boiling in the fat of the duck for two-and-a-half to three hours, so they are cooked well enough, as the peasants would say, that a piece of straw can pass right through the meat.

The carcasses, twelve a week, are consigned to a stock: roasted for a good colour, and put in a pan with enough cold water to cover, a bottle of white wine, leeks, carrots and garlic, and skimmed and simmered for two hours. The stock is then sieved and clarified, using a mix of fresh onions, leeks, carrots, tomatoes, offcuts from other meats to hand and three egg

THE INFLUENCE OF THE ROUX
BROTHERS FROM 1968

Since the opening of Le Gavroche, originally in Sloane Street and later in Upper Brook Street, the Roux brothers have initiated a generation of restaurants. Some, like Gavvers and Les Trois Plats, remain integral parts of the business. Others, most importantly Tante Claire, have since gone independent or chefs such as Rowley Leigh, Marco Pierre White and Christian Delteil have set up on their own. Stars are Michelin ratings from different years.

☆☆☆	☆☆☆
LE GAVROCHE (Albert)	THE WATERSIDE INN (Michel)

☆	☆☆
POULBOT KENSINGTON PLACE (Rowley Leigh)	TANTE CLAIRE (Pierre Koffmann)
☆ MAZARIN (René Bajard)	☆☆ HARVEYS (Marco Pierre White)
☆ PARIS HOUSE (Peter Chandler)	☆ L'ARLEQUIN (Christian Delteil)
☆ INTERLUDE DE TABAILLEAU (Jean Louis Tallaibeau)	☆ LES ALOUETTES (Michel Perraud)

LES TROIS PLATS
GAVVERS
GAMIN
ROUXL BRITANNIA

whites, cooked for an hour to form a crust and clear. The whole duck translates into two dishes. The first involves five parts of the bird, each cooked and sauced differently but arranged in a circle round the plate.

PALETTE DE CANARD EN CINQ VARIATIONS

1. THE ROAST BREAST: Take off the magret and roast pink. Set aside the meat and sweat a diced shallot in the pan, deglaze with Spanish vinegar and a little duck stock to form a clear sauce, which is the principal sauce of the plate.

Serve the breast on *pommes dauphin*: the potatoes grated, squeezed dry, placed in a small pan with some oil, pressed down over a slow, slow flame and turned over when crisp.

2. THE THIGHS: Sweat a good measure of onions and garlic with a little carrot. In another pan, brown the outside of the thighs in oil to get a good colour. Add to the onions and garlic with a bouquet garni, top up with a big country wine like a Rioja, and braise for 1–2 hours. Take out the thighs. Adjust the wine for a sauce, and finish with a little butter. This sauce is for the thighs, served on a clump of egg noodles.

3. CONFIT OF LEGS: Take the confit of leg out of the fat, and steam gently through. Place in a hot oven to crisp the skin. Serve on a salad of 3 or 4 mixed leaves, dressed with a vinaigrette of Dijon mustard and oil.

4. THE STUFFED NECK: Take the bone out of the neck and tie up 1 end with string. Fill the rest of the neck with a stuffing of trimmings from the duck, a little pork, breadcrumbs and mushrooms. Tie up the end. Cook slowly in the duck fat. Serve on a bed of lentils cooked in good stock, made with bayonne ham shins and herbs.

5. THE FOIE GRAS: Pan fry a slice of foie gras. Steam a cabbage leaf and wrap the foie gras inside the cabbage.

Where confit and foie gras are often portrayed as the villains of so-called healthy eating, leadweights that anchor diners to their chairs along with cream and butter, here is an acute example of a kitchen that has imposed its sense of design and proportion to achieve a dish with balance. The sauces are no longer the flour and butter compositions they would have been in classical cooking, but have become clear statements, almost devoid of fat. The cooking has changed.

The stock has another role that provides an equally spectacular main course.

DUCK CONSOMMÉ WITH LOBSTER

THE LOBSTER: Take a live Scottish lobster and place it in the warm duck stock. Bring to a very gentle simmer, and set aside on the corner of the stove to cook slowly for 10 minutes. Remove the lobster and clean out of the shell. Sieve the consommé.

THE VEGETABLES: Take a mix of colourful vegetables: leeks, carrots, French beans, peas, broad beans. Cut to equal sizes, turn in butter, and poach in the duck consommé.

TO SERVE: Put the lobster pieces and vegetables back into a soup tureen. Add some thin slices of the confit of giblet and heart.

The soup might be served with scallops, a ravioli of seafood, or wild mushrooms.

GREAT
DISGUISES

—

FAT AS AN ISSUE

FOIE GRAS

FOIE GRAS WAS the supreme fat, the personification of a style of cooking whose wheels and axles are the butter and lards of the north, and the oils of the south.

'The goose is nothing, but man has made of it an instrument for the output of a marvellous product, a kind of living hothouse in which grows the supreme fruit of gastronomy,' wrote C. Gerard, in *L'Ancienne Alsace à Table*.

The Egyptians reared geese and ducks for their livers. So did the Romans. The Hungarians encouraged neighbouring countries through the cold war to develop production to supply western capitals.

But goose is in season only from October to February, while ducks can be raised through the year.

WARM ENOUGH TO PUT A HAND IN THE OVEN

A goose liver is sweeter, mellower, more refined, larger, more ovoid than a duck liver. Opinions divide on the best. A good liver should weigh around 600–800g for goose; 300–600g for duck. Some weigh more, but not necessarily to the good.

A liver should be creamy white, tinged pink. It likes strong seasoning. The oven should be warm enough to put a hand in, and the fat in which it cooks ought to be touchable. The taste matures if allowed to rest for a few days. Eighty per cent of the work in making a terrine is in choosing the foie gras. Variations on the theme abound, some wrapped in white fat, others with a jelly of Sauternes. This definitive version is from Michel Bourdin at the Connaught Hotel in London. It is served on its own trolley.

Bourdin uses livers from the Landes. They are taken out of the ice and *sous vide* packing, and allowed to warm to room temperature, when they become more malleable. The flesh is soft and resistant, so it springs back to its original shape when squeezed. The twin lobes are separated, their gossamer skin scraped off, and the arterial vein stripped out and set aside. The liver is laid out and flattened gently with the side of the hands, like working dough, seasoned with a mix of pepper, salt, nutmeg, saltpetre and dampened with a tablespoon of white port and one of old Madeira. Brandy is too strong. The livers marinate overnight.

The next day, they are packed inside a terrine. Half-way up, a line of black Périgord truffles, pared back to fat pencil lengths, are run through the centre. The top is filled up with more liver. This parcel is then sealed inside a vacuum pack (*sous vide* was developed originally for foie gras for the Troisgros Brothers at Roanne), and baked in a bain-marie for fifty-five minutes. It must be cooked through, or else when it is left to mature for up to two weeks, the bacteria will activate.

The loaf is unsealed and its layer of buttercup yellow fat is scraped off. The inside is smoothed with the side of a hot knife and decorated with more shards and circles of truffle.

The terrine is served with a port jelly:

Add two-thirds beef stock, one-third chicken stock to diced meats, carrots, onions, leeks, bouquet garni, 16 egg whites, and port. Bring to a simmer. Cook ½ hour to clarify. Strain. Add more port. Colour with cochineal and caramel to match the colour of ruby port.

The truffles and their shavings have been kept in a marinade of port, Madeira and brandy, which is used to flavour the stock and also poured over the port jelly before it is served.

COUNTRY VERSIONS

In Escoffier's kitchen, the foie gras was trimmed, studded with truffles, seasoned with salt and pepper, set over a heat to stiffen, washed with brandy, encased in caul, kept in a tightly shut terrine to mature, and only then wrapped in pastry and baked for forty minutes to the pound. In the dining-room, the waiter broke the pie crust and scooped out the foie gras with a spoon. Escoffier recommended noodles, macaroni, lasagne or rice with a little cream go beside the pâté, and/or sauces of chicken or veal stock, flavoured with port or sherry and finished with butter.

Similar country recipes are found in the Périgord, sometimes extended with an equal amount of pork fat. From around Cahors, comes a surprising recipe with capers. The foie gras is poached in white wine and Madeira seasoned with thyme and bay; macerated in the liquid overnight, then cut into steaks and sauced with equal amounts of velouté flavoured with Madeira, and double cream acidulated with lemon and capers.

Foie gras is a modern restaurant obsession, and has become what caviar and truffles were to the classical kitchen. The pan juices in which the fillets are fried are guarded for re-use, or else the livers are used secretly: wrapped inside a cabbage leaf with a pigeon breast; shavings inside a leek parcel with fillets of sole and a dressing of shallot and lime vinaigrette; or in an artichoke heart. In a sense, there are foie gras kitchens. A cynic might say that the advance of the post-war era was from chicken liver pâté to foie gras terrine.

As a centrepiece, foie gras dominates. Where the classical and country cooks preferred to make terrines and serve foie grass cold, the modern kitchen has gone over to hot. This recipe from Jean-Louis Dumonet captures the demarcation lines well.

DUO DE FOIE GRAS EN HABIT DE CHOUX
ET PANÉ À LA CIBOULETTE

1. Slice two equal steaks of foie gras of around 50g each. Season well on both sides. Poach a good-sized cabbage leaf and allow to cool. Wrap 1 of the livers in the leaf and steam for 2–4 minutes. 'The test is to feel it with the thumb: it must be slightly bouncy when pressing lightly upon it.'

2. Pan fry the second slice for 2 minutes on each side. Chop a bunch of chives and wipe the foie gras in them to dress. Deglaze the pan with cider vinegar and a drop of hazelnut oil.

TO SERVE: Place the cabbage-wrapped slice to one side of the plate, and garnish with rock salt and roughly ground pepper. Put the other slice opposite, and pour over the sauce. Garnish with a salad of lamb's lettuce dressed with a hazelnut vinaigrette.

BUTTER

B RITISH REGIONAL COOKING was dairy and livestock cooking. The fat of the animal was used to cook: the crust for mutton pies made with mutton fat; beef dripping for steak pies; lard for pork pies. Sandwiches of bacon fat were made with oatcakes or brown bread. Old English gravies were sometimes built up with dripping and fat, flavoured with some diced onion or herbs.

Butter was the first ingredient to hand, a first stop to warm the pan, or moisten the flour. It underwrote even the stocks.

These farmhouse butters would have been rough and ready, with English sweetcreams often being quite cheesy in themselves. The professional kitchen cleaned them by heating gently to a froth, taking off the heat, leaving to stand so the impurities sank to the bottom of the pan, then straining through muslin.

Clarified butters, like stocks, could be infused with new flavours. The cold butters in the classical kitchen were just as complex as the sauces.

Montpellier has the stamp of the hollandaise family. It was meant as a dressing for cold fish:

BEURRE MONTPELLIER

Blanch watercress, parsley, chervil, tarragon, chives and spinach. Refresh. Drain. Squeeze dry. Pound to a fine paste in a mortar with blanched shallot, gherkins, capers, clove of garlic, anchovy fillets. Mix in 10oz butter, 3 hard-boiled egg yolks, 2 raw egg yolks and finally 7 fl oz oil, as if making a mayonnaise. Sieve. Season with cayenne.

More familiar and simpler are the herb butters, of which *beurre maître d'hôtel* came to be an insignia.

BEURRE MAÎTRE D'HÔTEL

Work 9oz butter until soft. Add 1 tablespoon chopped parsley, salt, pepper and the juice of ¼ lemon.

Mustard was added, especially for grilled fish. The addition of two tablespoons of meat glaze and two of tarragon made *beurre colbert*. A reduction of red wine and shallots with a meat glaze creates a *marchand de vin*, classically for grilled meats, usually steak, but, oddly, a good suitor for broccoli.

Basil, tarragon and mint also respond well. So do nuts: shelled, roasted or blanched, skinned and pounded with a little water; fruits: the juice and a zest from the rind; and other aromatics like shrimps, garlic, soft roes, peppers, horseradish, smoked salmon, anchovies, in a ratio of roughly one to two; vegetables puréed and mixed in a ratio of one to one.

Such devices provide a different scale of seasonings to lift up different corners of a dish and provide hidden pivots.

OILS

UNLIKE BUTTER, WHICH remained central to the cooking, oil did not feature strongly in the classical kitchen. Oils tended to be dressings, separate from whatever they sauced, liquids that arrived towards the end of the cooking chain.

But for the modern kitchen, they offered another dimension. Pine, walnut, the potent hazelnut, were all brought into play. And, like stocks, oils could be vehicles for flavours and take on the role of sauces.

MACERATED OLIVE OIL

Chop finely a skinned and de-pipped tomato, ½ red pepper, 1 skinned clove of garlic, black and green olives, thyme, basil, blanched fennel, courgette, sautéed shallot, pepper, capers, saffron and salt. Mix, and cover with olive oil. Leave to macerate for 1–4 days.

FLAVOURED OLIVE OIL

Add ½ litre good white wine vinegar to two litres of olive oil. Add chopped carrots, celery, onions, leeks, fennel, red pepper. Season with a citrus fruit and herbs. Cook slowly for 1 hour. Take off the heat and leave to infuse for 1 hour. Strain and bottle.

In Britain, this use of oil was a new horizon altogether. Post-war, the only source of olive oil was the chemist. Entry into the EEC brought with it the oil culture of the south and, formidably, the virgin and extra-virgin oils that characterized the cooking of Tuscany and Provence. The market imposed itself on the kitchen.

But creams, butters and heavier fats did not lend themselves to innovative uses. They are disguises, the big wheels of a tractor that carve great grooves of flavour across dishes. Irrevocably, the movement has been to use them less and less. The logic of letting foods taste of themselves leads incontrovertibly towards the complete shedding of the inessentials.

THE TURNING POINT: NON-STICK PANS

T**HE MODERN KITCHEN** evolved to the point where fats could be side-stepped. The idea that there might be no fat, no oil and no lard at all, and that a meat or fish might just cook, as in grilling, straight on the pan or the hot steel, followed from the dismantling of dishes. The non-stick pan offered the ultimate flavouring option: zero.

The first step in splitting the cooking process completely had been reached. Where the classical kitchen had sought to integrate every aspect of the cooking, the modern kitchen considered every aspect separately. The technique and knowledge that ran through the *Guide Culinaire* had been traced back to the very root.

A number of people closed in on this point at roughly the same time. Michel Guérard's *Cuisine Minceur*, published in the early Seventies, is as good a textbook on modern techniques as exists, although at the time he was still looking for substitutes to conventional cooking, swapping cream for fromage frais. Ten years later, Anton Mosimann, then at the Dorchester in London, unveiled his *Cuisine Naturelle*. He poached or boiled meats, and brought in combinations of herbs to compensate. Others had also gone down this road less overtly, notably Raymond Blanc in England, Alain Senderens in Paris. Here was a discernible stage on from the heritage of Lyons.

Bérnard Loisseau is part of this group. He already had two stars in Michelin in 1982, when he began to change his cooking. Loisseau has the stocky frame of a rugby player, the round features of a monk, and a conviction, not just in his own talent, but in the principles he applies. He comes from the Auvergne, trained with the Troisgros brothers at Roanne and then worked in Paris. In 1975 he took over the Côte D'Or at Saulieu, which, since the death of Alexandre Dumaine eleven years previously, had fallen back. '*T here comes a point with cooking when you have to say, you just cannot go any further. What is the point? You cook a stock for three days and all for a little puddle on the plate. You use tens of different ingredients. And all to achieve what? Cooking had reached a point where you needed a dictionary to know what all the different herbs and ingredients were. But things should taste of themselves, and that is enough. There is a medium here. You cannot keep on throwing more and more ingredients at a dish and calling that cuisine.*

'So I went back to my grandmother's cooking. I took it apart. They are her recipes. But when my grandmother cooked a chicken in a pot, it was all together. You put the soup in a cup and you could see the rim of fat around the edge, but the bit you wanted was the dark juice at the bottom of the cup. That's what I set out to do, to take away all the fat and just serve the dark juices.

'In fact, my cooking is very simple – anyone could do it at home. Except . . . except that you cannot cook and be with your guests. Because this style of cooking has to be done to order. Every last piece put in place à la minute. That is one law. The other is that the products themselves must be of the highest quality.'

Instead of deglazing his roasting pans with wines, spirits and stocks, he uses only water. Rabbit, for example, is pot roasted in the traditional French style using a little butter, but when it is cooked the pan is scrupulously degreased and then deglazed with water. 'You do not need anything else. The sugars are all there in the pan. You only need to taste them – why cover them up with other things?'

To this end, he expanded the restaurant into growing its own produce. The gardener became as much a part of the kitchen team as the sous chef. Variety and freshness of ingredient became paramount.

Any fats used are taken off with absorbent paper. His was one of the first restaurants of note in France to introduce a menu of vegetable dishes, not strictly vegetarian, because meat and fish juices are used to season and flavour. In this menu, the roles have been reversed and the vegetables have taken the lead: a velouté of caramelized cauliflower; roast carrots dressed with the juices from a veal roast; a courgette galette sauced with the juice of sea urchins; a ragoût of celeriac scented with truffles; cheese and sweets.

The style pushed Loisseau into re-interpreting dishes. He takes, for example, an old dish of hot foie gras laid out on a bed of lentils, and turns it inside out, using just enough foie gras to season the lentils, reducing them to a purée, and serving them as a sauce for roast fillets of whiting, offsetting these two with a clump of deep fried onions. The interplay of the different tastes and techniques assumes a greater importance because the foods themselves, as in Japanese cooking, are almost naked. Seasonings have become strategic G-strings. There is no woolly jumper of fat to cover them up.

Fish dishes are often offset with vegetables: turbot with mashed potatoes, red mullet with a compote of olives, sea bream with a fondue of onions, scallops with chicory acidulated with apple.

GREAT BRITAIN, 1974
STARRED RESTAURANTS FROM
THE MICHELIN GUIDE

Michelin's arrival in Britain in 1974, brought a cautious assessment of one-star restaurants. Only six are still trading in the same form. The French influence is mandatory, exceptions being made only for the Chinese Lee Ho Fook and the one English bastion, Simpson's.

ENGLAND AND WALES

Town	Establishment
Bath	The Hole in the Wall
Bray	Waterside Inn
Brixham	Randalls
Canterbury	Duck Inn
Fressingfield	Fox and Goose
Hintlesham	Hintlesham Hall
Ilkley	Box Tree
Kildwick	Kildwick Hall
Manchester	French Restaurant
Swavesey	Hotel de la Poste
Tavistock	Horn of Plenty
Thornbury	Thornbury Castle

LONDON

City	Le Poulbot
Islington	Carriers
Kensington	Le Bressan
Kensington	Le Coq Hardi
Kensington	La Torque Blanche
Mayfair	Connaught
Mayfair	Le Gavroche
Soho	Lee Ho Fook
Strand	Simpson's-in-the-Strand

SCOTLAND

Glasgow	Malmaison

Perhaps this smacks of the zealot, the worthy rather than the elegant, but there is balance. There is still foie gras. There is still deep frying, but there is a successful sense of compromise and good sense, which allows the cooking to remain fluent.

Loisseau's signature is this soup of snails. It is a gesture of defiance, not just because the ingredients are essentially free, but because the snail has for centuries only been served in one way: drenched in garlic butter.

Nettles are in season when they reach the first flush of growth, once early in spring, and again in late summer. Only the top leaves are used, because the stalks become straw-like. Out of season, Loisseau freezes them. Blanched, they lose their sting and attain a green pepperiness.

SNAIL AND NETTLE SOUP AFTER
BÉRNARD LOISSEAU

Cook the snails for 30 minutes. Make a courtbouillon using the snail juice, a bouquet garni, 2 carrots, 2 large onions stuck with cloves, and 2 leeks. Take out the vegetables, and put them through a blender. Pluck 100g nettles, wash and blanch for 5 minutes. Drain and put them through a blender.

Warm 4 dozen snails in the courtbouillon. Add a soup spoon of the vegetable mix to act as a liaison, then add the nettles. Check the seasoning: 10g salt to 2g pepper (nettles are naturally peppery), and the juice of a lemon. Serve very hot.

Here is a deep sea change, a cuisine demonstrably different from what has gone before, and yet strong enough to stand on its own, with its own principles and tenets, effective for itself and relevant to its own time.

THE MIGRATION NORTH

—

VEGETABLES: THE AGENTS OF CHANGE

ONE OF THE great energies of cooking has come from *cuisiniers* crossing frontiers and being confronted with new food cultures. Loisseau, for instance, came out of the peasant areas of Auvergne and Lyons, and set about creating his own personal cooking.

The controlled and stylized classical cooking took its inspiration and beliefs from the north. It was about large indoor kitchens, serving an aristocracy and an affluent industrialized class. It was urban. It was focused on Paris and other capitals, but, equally, survived only in moneyed international climates.

Point's message about the quality of the ingredients appealed more to the ethos of southern cooking. Chefs unashamedly took their inspiration from the sun. Roger Vergé named his book *Ma Cuisine du Soleil*. The spirit was of the outdoors, of Point's garden terrace or, failing that, the conservatory.

Alain Chapel went further: 'Almost forgotten these days, but worthy of reinstatement, is the barbecue . . . you only have to eat small birds cooked on a skewer in the open air on a grill, to become an ardent convert.'

The same sense of re-discovery fills the first Elizabeth David books on Mediterranean and Italian cooking. This was an intellectual movement, a migration of thought south, after years of hibernation in the northern cities, and one which found a sympathetic echo on the other side of the world in California. Fortuitously, the mood has been matched by post-war opening up of world markets.

The agent of modern cooking has been, surely, the vegetable which for the classical cooking was a minor event, but for the modern kitchen is a motivator, offering the chance of new dimensions in which varieties and seasons become fundamental.

The vegetarian culture of the south has made swift inroads into the meat-oriented bastions of the north. Many reasons might be advanced for this: the need for trade, improved living conditions, less manual work, a taste for the exotic. England has been adopted into the culture of Europe.

THE EUROPEAN HOTHOUSE

The sweep of horticulture shadows the migration from equatorial jungle. There was no garden of Eden, or if there was, it might have been a small tropical oasis. The first settlers took with them their seed and animals and they too, like humans, had to adapt to survive.

Early Europe was forest. Primitive peoples hunted, killed and cooked, and supplemented this diet with the almost unimaginable leap that cereals could provide bread, and that olives gave oil. The southern European countries, notably Italy and Spain, were able to host vegetables from Asia: broad beans, basil, melon, cumin, lettuce and onion. And later came the same breadth of migration from south America: tomato, beans, peppers, aubergines, okra and, most importantly, potato. Southern Europe was already mother to the seasonings of European cooking: the celery, fennel, chervil, lovage, chive, dill, parsley, marjoram, chicory, mustard, garlic. Further north, roots and cabbages prospered. As with oil and butter, Europe divides on vegetables roughly around Lyons. The speed of modern transport and hot house technology bridge the geographical gap.

THE ENGLISH GARDEN

The English had always gardened where the French cooked. The walled gardens, the allotments, the cabbage patches became our perspective. Not, like the Dutch, on any commercial scale. Few market gardens survived the relentless rolling back of the cities. City suburbs were known for their vegetables: Enfield for cabbages, Shepperton for broccoli. Fulham, Chiswick and the Thames Valley were developed on the fertile ground that fed nineteenth-century Covent Garden.

A quirk of British nature meant that gardening, like fishing, was portrayed as an amateur enthusiasm, peripheral to the main stream of survival, which of course it could not have been, even in the nineteenth century. When Napoleon called the English a nation of shopkeepers, he probably meant it as a matter of fact. To a nation of cooks and restaurateurs, produce is fundamental; to the grocer it is optional, an item of trade, not survival.

Foreigners often chronicled the enormous amounts of meat eaten by the English, but their experience may have been of the autumnal glut, and at other times of year meat was probably scarce. The first vegetable cultivations – parsnips, carrots, beets, turnips, mangolds – were meant to feed the animals first.

But in time, English cookery seems to have become accustomed to a supply of fresh vegetables from early March to Christmas. The most important job of the organized gardener, was somehow to ensure that there would be fresh vegetables to feed the people and livestock through the winter. Spring greenery was needed as early as possible to clear out the effects of months of a diet of cured meats and old storages. Not even kings were immune. Henry VIII had scurvy from a lack of vegetables in his diet. The first nettles in March would have been a welcome sight. This need for fresh vegetables dominated the year, in a northern climate that was conspicuously tougher than in the south, where the summer heats and droughts presented other problems.

As a result, even in a nation of meat eaters, vegetable cooking has come arguably to outstrip that of other countries.

Literary mentions of vegetables suggest a great renaissance around the sixteenth century. A slim volume called A *Short History of Agriculture* by Philpot, puts the appearance of the French bean, at 1509; parsley, 1518; globe artichoke, 1546; radish, 1547; pea, during the reign of Henry VIII; beetroot, endive, thyme, 1548; turnip, 1550; leeks, 1557; carrot, 1558; lettuce, 1562; spinach, 1568; rhubarb, sage, 1573; onion, during the reign of Elizabeth I. But this rather convenient picture may have more to do with the spread of printing presses, rather than some sudden upsurge in imports. Monasteries and manors had organized cultivations before then.

MEAT AND TWO VEG

Northern countries were often able to grow vegetables more successfully than southern. Even if the vegetables were not indigenous, they grew more happily in the rich, wet soil, than in the hard-baked ground of the Mediterranean. The French might point to their cabbages, even aubergines, certainly tomatoes, although borrowed from Italy; but in terms of variety and invention across the spectrum, the English kitchen is remarkable. The two vegetables of 'meat and two veg', are a cruel image of a powerful side of the cooking.

It does not seem unreasonable to suppose that the feudal cottager and Victorian gardener held the true treasure house of English cooking as it might have been, if only from the circumstantial evidence that this was where most individual effort was directed. The arrival of French cooks and their methods did not impress W. Robinson, editor of *The Garden* in 1885, who declared: 'Even when he gives us French beans, they swim in butter. The French cooks, supposed to be the best, systematically make the natural flavours of the many delicate vegetables of their markets, secondary to that of butter – now alas, often mere grease or hardened oil.'

Early accounts of market gardening paint a shambolic picture of lost varieties and seed types, broken only by occasional estate husbandry. Even 100 years ago, details like types and varieties were difficult to find in any consistent form. Commercial rivalry, sloppy record-keeping and the limits of locality penned in the development. Unlike vines, where the idea that one grape could produce a different wine to another was established, the thought that one carrot might be different from another remained largely unexplored.

But as the supporting cast, English vegetable cookery stands out and retains a taste of the earth, even as the urban sprawl rolls onward like some fat man who cannot stop himself falling all over the countryside.

TOVEY'S INNOVATIONS

As with fish, the kitchen has deliberately shortened cooking times. Vitamins and fibre survive. Tastes are offset with seasonings and herbs. With the beginning of the global market in the Sixties, the kitchen suddenly had a great harvest at its doors. John Tovey perhaps saw the potential for this abundance first, and took it forward. Tovey was a theatre man, who turned late to cooking. He adapted a beautiful house on the shores of Windermere as a hotel, and employed the English boarding house system of set meals at set times, and no choice before the sweet. But if there was no choice, he compensated by offering seven courses, and in each one an array of different tastes. Main course meats arrive surrounded by different vegetables, each one seasoned, spiced, transformed. With an April roast loin of pork stuffed with apricot and hazelnuts and served with a gin and orange sauce he served glazed carrot with ginger, mashed swede with horseradish, toasted parsnip, French beans, grated beetroot cooked in walnut oil, red cabbage with garlic and juniper, and glazed potatoes. Meat with seven veg. Seventeen flavours on a plate may be excessive, but here was a concept of variety. Like Point, Tovey changed the menu every day.

In early March, a loin of Lakeland lamb, now nearly a year old, is roasted and served with a redcurrant and caper sauce, surrounded by mange-tout, deep fried curried salsify, diced swede with honey, glazed carrots with Pernod, broccoli with hollandaise, French beans and minted potatoes.

SOUPS

THE THEME IS found again, and as influentially, with soups. The combination vegetable soup has become as much a mark of the modern English restaurant kitchen as the consommé, the brown Windsor or mock turtle was to the classical menu.

Rustic farmhouse soups of simmered onions, braised vegetables, stock or water are barely any different from a vegetable stock or, for that matter, the cullises of early cooking. Their revival may have had much to do with the invention of the food processor. Vegetable mills used to purée soups before then were messy, unforgiving contraptions to clean.

Taking combinations of different vegetables, spices and even fruits is a singularly English tactic. Sometimes there are just two elements: leek with chicory, mushroom, coriander, lemon balm or watercress; broad bean with mushroom, toasted almond, cashew nuts or watercress; carrot with apple, coriander, ginger or orange.

Farmhouse recipes added water to the braised vegetables. Tovey favours introducing stock – usually a light chicken – at the end. The soups improve with keeping, as the tastes weld. The proportions are a pint of stock to a pound of vegetables and a quarter-pound of onions and other aromatics.

JOHN TOVEY'S BASIC SOUP

Slice onions. Brown slowly in butter. Add the diced vegetables. Brown. Moisten with a good measure of sherry and/or water. Cover tightly with foil, both over the bed of vegetables and under the lid to seal in the juices. Cook 10–40 minutes. Liquidize with the stock/milk/cream.

This workaday formula has served restaurants well with only mild embellishments, a few herbs strewn across the top, the mandatory wiggle of cream, a slurp of alcohol. Different ingredients can be mixed, or old country dishes restated in new ways:

CAULIFLOWER CHEESE SOUP AFTER

JOHN TOVEY

Sweat 4oz diced onions in butter. Add 2lb diced cauliflower. Deglaze with sherry. Cover with foil, and seal up the lid with foil. Braise for 20 minutes. Add the stock. Liquidize. Reheat with 4oz mature Cheddar.

Sally Clarke's one-woman show among the antique shops of Kensington Church Street has illuminated the west London eating-out scene for much of the Eighties, bringing in ideas from the west coast of America and changing the menu twice a day. Her style is relaxed but no less rigorous, and makes free use of the modern market.

SOUP OF ROAST YELLOW PEPPERS WITH SAGE AND PARMESAN, SERVED WITH GRILLED TOASTS OF TOMATO, RED PEPPER AND SAGE

THE SOUP: In a wide, heavy-based pan heat olive oil with 4 crushed cloves of garlic and 1 tablespoon chopped sage. Stir with a wooden spoon until the aroma is released, but do not let the garlic burn. Add 1 finely chopped onion, 3 sticks chopped celery, chopped fennel, a small chopped green chilli with the seeds, and 6 yellow peppers diced to 1-inch squares. Stir over a high heat until the vegetables soften. Salt. Just cover with vegetable stock or water, bring to a boil. Place in a hot oven gas 7, 425°F (220°C) uncovered and bake 20–30 minutes until the edges of the vegetables have coloured. A few burnt patches improve the flavour. Take out and liquidize, adding more water or stock to make smooth. Sieve through a medium/fine sieve into a clean pan. Season. Heat gently, and serve in warm plates with Parmesan shavings and drizzled olive oil.

THE TOASTS: Preheat the grill. Put a quartered red pepper on the grill, skin side up, and cook until the skins are black. Place in a bowl and cover to steam cool. Peel the pepper quarters carefully, and cut each piece in half, across the diagonal. Drizzle with a little olive oil taken from ¼ pint, and season with salt and pepper. Warm the rest of the oil with a crushed clove of garlic. Do not over-heat. Strain and add 1 teaspoon of chopped sage.

TO SERVE: Brush 4 slices of good fresh bread with the oil, and grill until golden. Turn over and place a slice of tomato on each, then a layer of pepper, then tomato, then pepper. Season with salt and pepper. Drizzle with more oil and grill again. Serve immediately with the soup, garnished with sprigs of fresh sage.

This unusual fruit soup takes the English respect for wine, adds the traditional fruits of a summer pudding and goes further, to make use of exotics.

CLARET SOUP AFTER GARRY HOLLIHEAD

THE SOUP: Mix 1 bottle claret; 1 bottle light, sweet Muscat; 6 juniper berries; a punnet each of blackcurrants, blackberries, redcurrants and blueberries; a stem of ginger. Simmer slowly for 2–2½ hours. Liquidize. Strain through muslin. Chill.

THE GARNISH: Peel and dice 2 mangoes and 2 papayas. Scoop out the fruit from a dozen passion fruit. Add some hawthorn berries. Stone and slice 5 plums. Place a 2-inch ring in the centre of the soup plate and fill with the fruits, arranging the slices of plum on the outside. Scatter over a few hawthorn berries.

TO SERVE: Pour the chilled soup over the fruits from a skillet at the table.

From further south, comes this rather bijou idea from Provence.

HOT VEGETABLE TEA WITH ICED PISTOU
AFTER JACQUES MAXIMIN

THE VEGETABLES: Wash, trim, dry and grate separately equal amounts of carrot, celeriac and turnip. Slice the same amount of leek. Place each on their own trays in the bottom of the oven overnight to dry. Crush the vegetables to a powder and tie up in small, individual tea bags.

THE PISTOU: Boil 4oz garlic for 15 minutes. Remove. Dry. Purée with olive oil and basil and place in a sorbetière to make tiny balls of pistou sorbet.

THE TEA: Infuse one or two of the tea bags in boiling water. Serve with the pistou balls added at the last moment.

THE TRIMMINGS ON THE TREE

To the classical kitchen, vegetables were jewellery, standardized garnishes that barely merited menu descriptions of their own. There would be peas, à la francaise; there would be carrots, glacée. There was no reminder of the cottagers' fight to ensure a regular supply. This was an area which the professional felt happy to leave to the domestic cook. The whole rich heritage of French peasant cooking of, say, cabbage, did not translate.

But doing away with fats and bringing the produce to the fore led, perhaps unconsciously, to the reassertion of the vegetable. The cliché of the nouvelle cuisine of serving one or two carrots, or a few infant broad beans, was imbued with a sense of re-discovery. Here were foods that had not been properly appreciated before, and with which the modern kitchen could experiment.

From bit-part players, frowned on for their working class origins, vegetables came to be seen as a means of providing contrast, releasing the load that had been placed on the heavy, intense sauces; of lightening the cooking and bringing in a further index of options.

In some cases, such as the brussels sprout, the vegetables had hardly been developed to form any substantial trade. Early vegetable cooking was dominated by a small number of species.

ONIONS

THE ONION, WHOSE origins go back so far to middle Asia that they are lost, was as fundamental to European cooking as stocks were to the professional kitchen. Onions were the base on which all else was built, their use as instinctual for the cook as reaching for the butter. The smaller shallot was prized for its delicate seasoning, but other strains became the great extenders of flavours, the partner for any passing ingredient. They swam in the depths of the cooking. As with stocks, they were integral; literally, in soups and in gratins; partly so, in pies, tarts and in these white sauces.

ENGLISH WHITE ONION SAUCE FOR MUTTON

Peel and quarter 4 onions. Simmer in milk until soft. Strain and reserve the milk. Chop the onions. Thicken the milk with a flour and butter roux. Stir in the onions. Season with salt, pepper and nutmeg.

SAUCE SOUBISE (TRADITIONAL FRENCH)

Sweat ½lb thinly sliced onions in butter gently until they turn yellow. Dust with flour. Season. Add ½ pint veal or beef stock, or milk. Simmer 15 minutes. Sieve.

Compare such old-fashioned approaches to this vibrant regional relish, revived by Michel Guérard, for an onion marmalade to stand alone in the English way.

ONION MARMALADE AFTER MICHEL GUÉRARD

Brown 1½lb sliced onions in butter. Season with salt, pepper and sugar. Cover. Soften for 30 minutes, stirring occasionally with a wooden spoon. Add 7 tablespoons sherry vinegar, ¼ pint red wine and 2 tablespoons of grenadine for colour. Simmer on for another 30 minutes.

A more conspicuous role has been taken by the carrot.

CARROTS

Like anise, caraway, chervil, savory, coriander, cumin, dill, fennel and parsley, carrots are part of the *umbelliferae* family. But the leaves are bitter and brackenous, and peripheral to cooking. The women of court in the seventeenth century wore them on their sleeves as feathers.

The wild carrot is found in Greek and Roman cooking. These would have been gangly, white roots. The blush orange-red strains familiar today, trace their ancestry back down the old Moor trade routes, through Spain, across north Africa, to a purple-stained species found in Afghanistan. They were cultivated probably first in Holland, and arrived in England around 1600. The colonists took them to America.

Early recipes exploited their colour and sweetness. Before the sugar trade they were an able substitute, and were used in tarts, puddings and charlottes.

CARROT CAKE AFTER JOHN EVELYNE 1699

Grate 1lb breadcrumbs for 2lb carrot. Add ½ pint fresh cream or milk, ½lb butter, 6 new laid eggs (taking out 3 of the whites), ½lb sugar, salt, nutmeg, spice. Put in a buttered pan. Set in a 'quick' oven for an hour.

Classical cooks also came to underline their sweetness.

GLACÉ CARROTS

Scrub the carrots clean. Cut into equal parts. Dissolve 1 tablespoon sugar and a knob of butter into a wide pan of boiling water that will cover three-quarters of the carrot. Cook uncovered, so the liquid reduces to a syrupy glaze by the time the carrots are cooked through.

Escoffier saw this as the 'basic method, whatever the use'. Other cooks have followed, altering only perhaps the sugar for honey, or changing the shapes according to fashion, from dry, grated cook-downs, to circular discs, to turned ovals, mousses and matchsticks. Escoffier suggested only two developments: add boiling cream to infuse with the juices; and garnish generously with chopped parsley. Vichy usually claims the recipe for the spa's interest in health rather than sweet things, but the idea that only Vichy mineral water can be used smacks of commercial marketing rather than culinary sense.

Even wild carrots have often been credited with health-giving properties. The old wives' tale of helping people to see in the dark, stems from their richness in vitamin A, beneficial to the eyes, tonsils, liver and genitals, as a general diuretic. The vitamins gravitate towards the outer skin of the carrot, hence the advice to scrape and not peel. The skins, especially of older, larger carrots, were often re-used in stocks and stews, making nutritious additions even when they had lost the bright guards-man looks of early summer's first thinnings.

Classically, carrot soup was a thick, filling liquid. Potage Crécy (named after the chalky fields where Edward III's archers fought, and also the region better known for its Brie) was bulked out with rice, potatoes, cream and egg yolks. The flavour was either sweated out with onions at the start, or infused into the stock in the middle of the cooking. The modern kitchen has moved the carrot up to the front of the cooking, and flirted with it as thickener for sauces, taking over from cream or butter. The purée lends colour, texture and sweetness to a stock of, say, mussels with dill.

WITH BEEF

The global market has blurred the distinction between young and old. The restaurant kitchen has come to use almost solely young carrots, sautéed in a little butter, and served with one of the other umbelliferous herbs. But in bourgeois and regional cooking, the carrot's profile was a part of the winter scene.

It combines easily with other roots: turnip, celeriac, parsnip. Beef is its most common ally, like parsnip a frequent companion in a roasting tray, or else boiled for Victorian English cooking's symbolic dish.

The meat was typically salted, either silverside, brisket or topside, or, in Victorian terms, edgebone, soaked in clean water to wash out the unabsorbed brine.

BOILED BEEF AND CARROTS

Place the soaked joint in a casserole of cold water. Season with onion, parsley, clove, bay. Bring to a simmer. Cook for 1 hour to the pound. Scrub slightly less carrots to the pound than beef. Add the carrots for the final hour of cooking. Traditionally, this was served with a sharp sauce of horseradish.

Throughout the French regional variations on a daube of beef, the carrot shows its versatility. It figures at each stage of the cooking: diced as a base to be sweated off in fat along with onions and the meat itself; lending sweetness to the deglazing; as an aromatic along with other herbs and spices to flavour a young broth (sometimes substituted by tomato, in southern recipes); and as a vegetable in its own right, but for preference cooked in stock. In early English cooking, it was often served in gravy. The classical kitchen served it with a meat glaze.

WITH PORK

Pork can be an equally accommodating bedmate. These two recipes make use of the sweetness of the fat off cheap cuts:

PORK WITH LENTILS AND CARROTS

Soak red lentils. Scrub the carrots and slice lengthwise. Cook carrots and lentils together in stock at a slow simmer, for 1½ hours. Roast a belly of pork separately. Carve the pork, and lay in the bed of lentils to infuse for 20 minutes.

PORK WITH CARROTS

Slice a belly of pork into strips. Scrub and slice carrots. Brown onions in a pan. Pack the carrots and pork down tightly in the bottom of the pan. Add a little stock. Cover with foil and a lid. Cook slowly for 1½ hours.

WITH CITRUS FRUITS

Stronger spices like ginger, cinnamon, nutmeg, pepper and even horse-radish, are commonly found in older cooking: slaking a béchamel; uplifting mashes, bakes and custards.

Citrus is another seemingly unlikely, but widely used, companion. The acidulation of carrots is a feature of cooking that goes further south than traditional demarcations, and seems to follow a westerly trade route up from Africa.

FRANCE: Scrub the carrots. Cook in equal quantities of white wine, white wine vinegar and water. Make a vinaigrette of Dijon mustard and the cooking liquor. Marinate for up to 3 days.

SPAIN: Dress boiled carrots in an emulsion of garlic, oregano, coriander, pepper, orange or lemon juice and olive oil. Marinate for 2 days. Finish with chopped parsley.

MOROCCO: Simmer the carrots with garlic. Season with cinnamon, cumin, lemon, sugar, salt. Chill. Serve with oil and parsley.

Another Moroccan variation uses raw carrots, grated and macerated for an hour in orange flower water, lemon, sugar and salt.

By this yardstick, England's contribution is simply to grate the raw carrots and serve them as they stand. A depressing aspect, but the innovative cookery writer Nathalie Hambro has picked up the north African theme with this salad. The garnish is currants steeped in orange juice.

NATHALIE HAMBRO'S CARROT SALAD

Grate the carrots. Grate ginger. Dress both with olive oil and the juice of an orange. Macerate 2 hours.

John Tovey varies the idea again, by using walnut oil and stir-frying the grated carrots. In Provence, there is a regional dish of grated carrots and tomatoes, shallow fried in olive oil.

PARSNIPS

JUST AS THE carrot was cultivated in the middle ages as much to feed animals as humans, so was the parsnip. It managed the short journey across into domestic cookery through other values than just its nutritional worth.

It was valued for its sweetness, going to make wines, ales, even honey. The woody core of the older plants was thrown out, and the sweeter flesh puréed and mixed with mead for a sauce for fish. Dried and ground, parsnips were mixed one-third to two-thirds with wheat flour in the seventeenth century, and baked to make cakes.

The parsnip is a traditional accompaniment to roast beef, cooked alongside the meat in the dripping. The dairy link recurs with cream.

BAKED PARSNIPS (TRADITIONAL)

Slice parsnips and lay in a dish alongside carrot or pear. Cover with cream. Season with nutmeg and butter. Bake for ½ hour in a medium oven.

Puréed and creamed, the parsnip takes well to toasted, nutty seasonings like roasted pine kernels or sesames. The blanketing sweetness is well-coloured by militant spices like ginger, nutmeg and cumin.

Their traditional role overlooks the fact that the younger vegetables can be treated more gently.

STIR-FRIED PARSNIPS AFTER ANTON MOSIMANN

Sauté a handful of sesame seeds in a non-stick pan; add diced parsnip. Season with spring onions and garlic. Quick fry for 5–8 minutes. Add a few mange-tout for colour for the last 3 minutes. Season.

CELERY

THE GENTLE FLAVOUR of celery has come to make up a fundamental aspect of modern vegetable cookery, an almost mandatory addition to stocks and, as such, a premier seasoning. The leaves place it half-way between a herb and a vegetable, while the stalks offer a more resilient taste. It is a fine soup in itself, but also able to support other strong flavours like fennel; fruits like pear; or pick out herbs like lovage or dill.

In English cookery, celery was used with the stock from a boiled turkey to make a sauce. This recipe from Devon to accompany roast duck stands the test of time:

POTTED CELERY (TRADITIONAL, DEVON)

Pare and core 1lb apples. Cook with a little water and butter to a purée. Season. Wash and separate the celery stalks. Stand the celery in a tall pot, pour on the apple purée. Trim the celery so it is covered, and pack the rest in down the sides. Braise in a low oven for 2 hours.

The slow bakes of regional cookery bring out the earthy, floral flavours. Although this is a modern recipe used by Guy Savoy, its parentage is obviously regional:

BRAISED CELERY AFTER GUY SAVOY

Wash and trim the celery. Cut the stalks into 2-inch pieces. Blanch in boiling water. Drain. Warm some oil in a casserole and sweat onions and carrots. Add the celery. Season. Cover with stock or water. Add a knob of butter. Braise for 45 minutes in a medium oven.

CELERIAC

CELERIAC IS PART of the same family, first grown at the beginning of the nineteenth century. It has always seemed the poor relation of the root family, omitted completely from many books, rather ungainly and large, rough-skinned compared to turnips; overly pungent and pervasive compared to the parsnip; inclined to wateriness and provoking flatulence.

Even so, French cooks have happily used it to sauce fish; as gratins; in chips, croquettes or pan fried as a substitute for potato; or steamed and seasoned with lemon, thyme, honey, apple. In at least two incarnations, it has come to be characteristic of French cooking. It should be boiled with the skin on, and peeled afterwards.

CELERIAC PURÉE

Boil equal amounts of celeriac and potato. Drain. Peel. Add a good measure of butter and a slurp of olive oil. Mash or liquidize.

CELERIAC REMOULADE

Cut the celeriac into quarters. Blanch in water, acidulated with vinegar or lemon. Drain. Peel. Grate. For the dressing, mix anchovy fillets, garlic, chopped cooked shallots, mustard, capers, parsley and chervil with a little vinegar. Add an egg yolk, and pour in olive oil as for a mayonnaise.

On its own, celeriac needs vibrant, tough seasonings. John Kenward, at his restaurant in Lewes, often cooks the same food in two different ways and then brings both together on the plate.

CELERIAC AND GINGER AFTER JOHN KENWARD

Halve a celeriac. Cut away the skin. Dice one half, and simmer with onion, garlic, ginger, mace and lemon until soft. Drain, and purée with butter. Meanwhile, take the other half and slice into strips. Shallow fry with ginger and butter. Serve the two, side by side.

John Tovey creates this strident dish for serving in small quantities. The horseradish is best grated briefly, for one spin in a covered food processor, or the fumes are head-blowing.

STIR-FRIED CELERIAC WITH HORSERADISH

Halve a celeriac. Slice away the skin. Grate. Squeeze the juice of a lemon over the celeriac and marinate. Peel and grate a small horseradish. Stir-fry together.

BRUSSELS SPROUTS

B RUSSELS SPROUTS ARE a modern vegetable, developed in the last century. In 1885 there were only two varieties, now there are hundreds. The memory of mass-catered, flaccid green balls, the leaves still sodden and, in the centre, a little squirt of old, tepid vegetable water has spurred the modern kitchen to change the sprouts' natural shape.

Grated raw, their crisp leaves add texture to winter salads or can be steamed and seasoned like cabbage. Puréed, they lend a weight of nutritious vegetable, either for a soup or mixed with a quarter the amount of cream and butter to make a purée.

Just as recipes for carrot and parsnip sought to underwrite their sweetness, so it is the nuttiness of the brussels sprout that sets one parameter.

STIR-FRIED BRUSSELS SPROUTS WITH

WALNUT OIL

Pick over the sprouts, discarding any discoloured or weak leaves. Grate. Blanch in boiling water. Dry. Heat a pan with walnut oil. Stir-fry the leaves for 3–5 minutes.

SIMMERED BRUSSELS SPROUTS WITH

CHESTNUTS

Take half as many chestnuts as you have sprouts. Nick the skins. Boil for 3–5 minutes. Take out and skin the chestnuts. Put the chestnuts into stock and simmer for around 1 hour. Clean and pare the sprouts. Add to the chestnuts for the last 5–8 minutes. Remove. Dry. Dice some bacon and fry in a pan. Add the brussels sprouts and chestnuts. Stir-fry.

BRUSSELS SPROUTS WITH ALMONDS
OR HAZELNUTS

Cover the nuts with boiling water for 3 minutes, then take out and squeeze out of the skins. Toast the nuts under the grill or in the oven. Pare and simmer the sprouts. Drain. Mix the sprouts with the nuts and lemon butter.

BRUSSELS SPROUTS WITH SESAME OIL

Quarter the sprouts. Simmer for 5 minutes. Drain. Toast some sesame seeds. Dress with sesame oil and a few sesame seeds.

BROAD BEANS

THE TRADITIONAL USE of broad beans in English cooking was in a casserole with salt pork. The soaked shoulder was placed in a pot with carrots, onions and turnips, seasoned with peppercorns, covered with cold water and cooked at a slow simmer for twenty-five minutes to the pound. The beans were added for the last twenty-five minutes to cook in the salty aromatic stock, perhaps in a bag, so they could be served on the side with a parsley sauce.

Earlier recipes concentrated economically on larger, older beans. They were often served with fish. If there was no stew or stock to cook them in, a sweet wine or cider was used. Long cooking times emphasize their mealiness.

Modern cooks have tended to ignore the parsimonious value of extending the vegetables, and focused on the young bean, still the size of a thumb nail. Being younger, the thick béchamel sauces so beloved of the classical kitchen are unnecessary. This interpretation on the old theme substitutes bacon for pork, a quick fry for a slow casserole, sorrel for parsley.

BROAD BEANS AFTER LYNDA BROWN

Cut some fatty bacon into shards the same size as the beans. Fry in their own fat until crisp, but not burnt. Set aside the bacon, and fry the beans in the fat for 3 minutes. Add chopped sorrel at the last minute. Combine and serve.

If the beans are young enough, they can contribute to a fine salad. The pungent herbs set off the silkiness of the beans.

BROAD BEAN SALAD

Steam the beans for 4 minutes. Make a vinaigrette with good virgin olive oil, wine and lemon. Chop a mix of herbs – parsley, chervil, savory, basil, mint – and add half to the vinaigrette. Dress the beans, and garnish with the rest of the herbs.

BEETROOT

THE SMELL OF hot beetroot is the smell of street markets on chill November days: London smogs, thick scarves, hoarse breath, red cheeks, wet nose, jacket potatoes to warm gloved hands, chestnuts at a warm brazier.

Beets are one of the oldest vegetables of northern Europe, a staple food crop for the animals. Their reputation has never been fully reinstated. Instead, they have been abused by being pickled or used as a colourant in commercial processes, even substituting for strawberries in some jams. Even in its best known incarnation as borscht, its role is stunning but cosmetic. Like Cinderella, it loses its colourful glamour in time. Ruby turns dirty brown with over-cooking.

The mythology that surrounds borscht deflects from the fact that it was a poor family's soup, an eastern European relation to boiled beef and carrots, or even to a southern minestrone.

There are sophisticated variations where the meat is taken out of the soup, minced, and cooked inside pastry and bread doughs; where the soup is clarified into a consommé. But the best way to understand and cook it, is to keep in mind its origins.

Borscht should evolve from one day to the next, and it is only modern ideas that have focused on the central stages as the climax. My grandmother was raised in Kiev, and this is the recipe she taught my mother. Quantities are optional, but variety is important. One of each kind of vegetable for every two-inch thickness of meat is a good yardstick.

BORSCHT AFTER MIRA BLANK

DAY ONE: Take a brisket of beef, the bigger the better, depending on the size of pot you have. Cover with cold water. Add carrots, onion, leeks, parsnip. Bring to a simmer. Skim as for making stock, which is what you are doing. Cook gently on the corner of the stove for 3–4 hours, so the beef is just undercooked. (The vegetables would have provided the night's rather thin dinner for a family, but have given up most of their worth in to the stock.) Take out the brisket. Allow to cool. Put the stock in the fridge.

DAY TWO: Trim any surplus fat off the brisket. Ladle the skin of fat off the stock and strain. Put the brisket back in the stock. Dice onion, carrot, leek, parsnip to equal sizes. Add to the stock. Peel raw beetroot, and dice to the same size. Add a potato. Simmer 30–40 minutes. Leave to stand. Taste, and season with lemon juice.

This would be served either as a soup garnished with soured cream; or else with the meat sliced thinly in the bottom of the plate, the soup poured over and drunk first and the meat eaten afterwards. In poor families this would have been quite a feast, which it is, and a complete meal, perhaps on a Sunday. But the soup in practice matures, and is better the day after.

DAY THREE: Warm through the rest of the soup, and add a quarter wedge of cabbage for each person. Simmer 20 minutes. Serve.

The beetroot has noble qualities of its own. The elusive smell of cooking beets is hinged to a deep taste brought out by long, slow, consistent cooking, either simmered or baked, wrapped in foil.

My mother grates the cooked beets and then stir-fries them with garlic; or served warm, they can be sliced thinly and dressed with walnut oil and basil as a salad.

But for all the modern French kitchen's boast about simplicity, it is quite capable of transcending the classical kitchen's subtleties. Michel Roux quips that this dish which he conceived – and it is a proper conception – with Alain Chapel for a dinner for the *Académie Culinaire* is 'not difficult, but at the same time not for the faint-hearted'. Two of the great staples of medieval cooking have been raised up to the peerage of restaurant cooking.

GELÉE D'UN EXCEPTIONEL POT-AU-FEU, RAIFORT REMOULADE ET CAVIAR BELUGA AFTER MICHEL ROUX

THE POT-AU-FEU: Put 2.3kg shoulder or leg of venison, 4.5kg shin of beef, 450g wild duck legs, and the bones and carcass of a hare in a large stockpot. Cover with water. Bring to the boil, skim and leave to simmer. Wash, but leave whole, 2 leeks, a head of celery, a head of garlic, 4 large carrots, 25g juniper berries, a large bouquet garni (to include thyme and bayleaf), and 2 onions, cut in half and burnt on the gas or electric ring. Add to the stock, and leave to simmer for at least 8 hours. Do not add more water. The stock will now be of good flavour. Pass it through a fine sieve, and leave to cool.

TO CLARIFY: Mince 900g hare or other game, 2 onions, 4 celery sticks, 2 carrots. Add 8 egg whites. Stir into the cool stock, bring back to the simmer and keep just under boiling point until a crust forms. Cook on for another 20 minutes, then pass the now clear stock through a muslin-lined sieve. Cool and season.

If the stock is not of full flavour, a second clarification may be necessary. If so repeat the process. Pour off a little of the stock into a bowl and refrigerate to test the setting consistency. It should be just holding. ('If the stock is not firm enough, add some leaves of gelatine to achieve this.')

THE BEETROOT CREAM: Cook a large beetroot in salted water until very soft. Skin. Purée until smooth. Take 3 dessertspoons of the purée and whisk together with 850ml double cream and four dessertspoons of *glacé de fond blanc* (eg veal stock) until the soft peak stage. Season.

TO SERVE: Pour approximately 125ml consommé into each plate and allow to set. Spread a neat circle of the beetroot cream on top. Grate a little fresh horseradish on top, and spoon on a little caviar. Garnish with chervil.

A SILENT
DISCIPLINE

—

DESSERT COOKING

MUCH OF THE overcomplexity of the classical cooking was the royal houses' insistence on great architectural stages on which to set their food. The edible parts took up only tiny fractions of table space, compared to their framing. This was Carême's great forte. He was arguably the greatest of confectioners. Escoffier, Point, both the Roux brothers, and Raymond Blanc were, and are, skilled *pâtissiers*.

In practice, the kitchen divides more deeply between the pastry and sweet work, and what goes before. The heat comes first. That is cuisine. The confection is set aside, in a different department, with different ovens. The values are of flour and water, of transformation, rather than the cut and thrust of dishes for earlier courses. The pastry area is cool and dry, white flours and sugars spread a hospital-style anaesthetic over the worktops. The work space is blocked off somehow from the hot and wet of the cuisine. The procedures are quiet, not the noisy spitting, hissing, and clanking of pans. The menace of open blades and burning metals is replaced with hand work on elegant slabs of marble.

The great pastry was all to do with the grand hotels. As they disappeared, so the dishes fell out of the repertoire and into specialist shops, which even Carême had tried before going into the world of diplomacy. In regional cooking, somehow, baking seemed to find another form of expression, not the restaurant, but the tea house, the coffee shop, the middle-European compromise of bar and cakes, the afternoon or day-time place. Separate disciplines as handed down from the medieval guilds lingered longest with desserts, and persist in the form of factory-produced gateaux, or specialist *pâtissiers* supplying wholesale.

Baking and pastry were fundamental parts of English cooking, fatally dislodged by the invention of the Chorley Wood Process for baking bread in the Sixties. A whole vocabulary of lardy cakes, stotty cakes, of meat pies fell into disuse. In the space of a very short time, one of the key pillars of our cooking was taken down and replaced with, well, what should we call it, nutrition, perhaps? Not cooking. The English pudding, the Sussex pond, bread and butter, treacle tart, jam roly-poly went with it, although it was a far greater heritage than anything that has since tried to replace it.

As if in revolt, many rural restaurants self-consciously went back to some of these recipes, which were both deceptively simple and successful. The Sticky Toffee Pudding is a transformation that appeared on menus as far apart as the two great Lakeland rivals, Miller Howe and Sharrow Bay, and as far south as the Carved Angel, where George-Perry Smith's partner Joyce Molyneux had otherwise begun to move her cooking into an increasingly modern idiom. Variations in the coffee, or in substituting apricots for dates or other dried fruits, do not deflect from the core of the recipe which is rooted in the tradition of baking that had previously been the major influence on domestic cooking. This recipe includes Camp coffee and golden syrup, as an echo of post-war British larders.

STICKY TOFFEE PUDDING

Heat the oven to gas 4, 350°F (180°C). Line a loose-bottomed cake tin with 2 layers of greaseproof paper. Cream 4oz butter with 6oz soft brown sugar. Beat 4 eggs lightly and then, bit by bit, whisk into the mixture. Add 8oz self-raising flour. Mix 1 teaspoon bicarbonate of soda with 2 tablespoons Camp coffee with half a pint of boiling water and pour over eight ounces of chopped, stoned dates. Mix. Allow to cool until tepid. Pour over the flour and butter mixture so the result is a well amalgamated thick liquid. Pour into the tin and bake for one and half hours.

The traditional accompaniment would have been cream, but at Miller Howe, John Tovey evokes another deeply British tactic of serving it with a butterscotch sauce he credits to Delia Smith.

BUTTERSCOTCH SAUCE

Heat a 1lb tin of golden syrup in a bain-marie to liquefy. Pour into a thick-bottomed pan, and blend in 3oz butter and 4oz soft brown sugar. Cook 10 minutes. Take off the heat and allow to go tepid. Stir in ¼ pint cream. Season with vanilla essence and stir to a smooth paste. Serve straightaway, or store in jars in the fridge.

For the most part, small restaurant kitchens were not big enough to cope with a proper pastry division. Budgets did not run to an extra pair of hands. The pastry chef needs a slightly altered focus of a craft, a certain feel in the hands that not everyone has, so that a pastry chef might be a cook, but not all cooks are good pastry chefs. He became a specialist, a hired gun, preferring the outlet of shops and middle men, and shunning the interface of the dining-room.

And his tendency to work through the dark hours of the night imposed yet another barrier to integration in the main stream.

Nouvelle cuisine arrived like a train without a guard's van: a few mousses; many sorbets, once the sorbetière arrived; a few sculpted fruits; something dusted in chocolate (because chocolate was deemed mandatory); or just bought in from somewhere else and, essentially, from other thinkings.

Regional cooking had its own local characteristic repertoire of sweets. The classical kitchen had its historic sculptures. The next ideas were borrowed, not from what had gone before in terms of desserts, but from the rest of the cuisine. Modern cooks brought the thinking of previous courses into the final act more thoroughly than ever before. Chefs had not trained in pastry, or, if they had, not for any length of time, and so they tackled the course in a fresh way.

At first, the results were predictably lame, but as menus evolved, so a new idiom emerged and with it, perhaps, the crystallization of where the modern kitchen was going. Just as much as the handling of vegetables was a dynamic and necessary mark of the modern kitchen, so, equally, the creative conception of a plated sweet revealed the new *ésprit*.

Popular opinion meant that the cream, which had supported the trollies since Escoffier, was out of favour, so was loading up the mousses with as much butter as was humanly digestible. Fruits were accepted, but easy.

Christian Delteil opened his L'Arlequin in Battersea with a *chaud-froid* of citrus fruits. Fashionable kiwi or perhaps grapefruit, looking for the acidity, were sautéed with green peppercorns and pepper, drained, plated, then placed in a sabayon and put under the grill to flash warm through. Working on an idea from Maximin, where a dish of scallops were curled up in a ring in the centre of the plate where they could be grilled, Delteil developed over a few years this four-dimensional dessert, imbued with all the elements of contrast that make up the modern cooking. The mix of the sabayon browns uniformly under the grill.

CHAUD-FROID OF RED FRUITS AFTER
CHRISTIAN DELTEIL

SABAYON: Whip 5 egg yolks, 100g sugar, 1 tablespoon water to a creamy texture, and place in the fridge. This will keep 2–3 days. Whip 1 tablespoon sabayon with an equal amount of sweetened double cream per serving.

SORBET: Mix 12 egg yolks with 250g sugar. Pour in 1 litre of hot, boiled milk, stirring to keep it at 82°F. Flavour with vanilla. Simmer 5 minutes, then cool swiftly through a series of 3 cold pans laid into larger pans of cold water. Add to the sorbet machine. Add 50ml raspberry *eau de vie* at the last minute. When nearly ready, add 100g *crème chantilly* (double cream whipped with sugar) to smooth the texture.

THE FRUIT: Wash the raspberries and pile inside a ring. Cover with the sabayon and place under the grill.

THE COULIS: Blend half raspberries, half strawberries, 300g sugar, the juice of 1 lemon.

TO SERVE: Encircle a cold plate with the coulis. Position a ring of sorbet in the centre. Using a spatula, take the raspberries out of the grill and position on top of the sorbet.

Where the classical kitchen fell over itself in its use of pastry, the modern kitchen is sparing and diligent. The virtuoso Alain Senderens cooks in a way that is intellectually demanding. He is above all a cook of ideas, and one of the kings of the new generation. Here, he pares the role of the pastry back to its finest, most fragile, thinness. This tart works for pears, but has to be prepared to order or their juices run and spoil the pastry. *Pâté brisée* is an alternative, but, again, it must be rolled thinly and the apples cut equally transparent. The garnish in his Paris restaurant Lucas Carton is deep fried and sugared apple peel round the edge of the plate, in which little leaves of fresh mint lurk.

TARTE BONNE FEMME FINE AFTER
ALAIN SENDERENS

THE PASTRY: Pre-heat the oven to gas 7, 425°F (220°C). Butter the surface of the pastry dish. Lightly flour the work surface, and roll out the pastry (*pâté feuilleté*) very thinly, to obtain a rectangle 40 × 30cm. Lift the pastry on top of the pastry dish, and spike with a fork so it does not inflate in the cooking.

THE APPLES: Core the Golden Delicious and cut in half, getting rid of the core, and then slice as thin as 1mm. Lay these round the pastry, overlapping so the pastry is completely covered.

THE COOKING: Cut 35g butter into 15–20 pieces and distribute them on the surface of the tart. Cook for 16 minutes, then lower the heat and cook on for 10 minutes.

Serve hot with *crème fraîche*.

The recipe specifies Golden Delicious. The French tradition for apple tarts was to look for acidity and use varieties with little juice: Reine de Reinette; an English King of Pippins; later in the year, a Reinette de Canada.

AN ABANDONED HERITAGE

Today, such details may seem like nit-picking. Yet it was on the availability of variety, that the Victorians built their cooking. Developing and growing different strains of apples was a matter of pride. At the end of the nineteenth century there were more than 3,000 types of apple in common use across England. Every county, and nearly every month, had its own characteristic foods.

There were specific apples for specific dishes. The first Codlins – Keswick, Manks, Lord Grosvenor and Early Victoria – rose up like soufflés when baked, but made poor fruits for tarts, and collapsed into watery, mean purées. The Golden Noble, which did not fruit until October, was used for pies. The Bramley was not planted on any scale until the start of this century, when its accommodating nature and the length of its acidity, which can last through to the spring, made it a dominating force, displacing Dumelows, Warners King, Wellington, Monarch and others. Some varieties, such as Queen of the Sauce, from Hereford, were kept especially for sauces.

Eating apples were held in the same regard. The successive seasons gave the Victorians the sense of variety and change in their diet, that is too often overlooked. There are enormous differences in the tastes of different apples, not just between families, like Cox or Russets, but between strains. The first apple of the season was a crisp, juicy Jennetting; Discovery has a hint of strawberry; St Edmunds Pippin is almost pear-like; Savoury James Grieve was sharp, but with a mushy, marrow-like texture. One needs to see these varieties side by side to appreciate the full breadth of what has been lost. Apples were the focal point at the end of dinner, and, in their heyday, around 1890, their values were argued over with the same vehemence as wines are today.

It is this variety that we have thrown away in the last forty years. Now, even the more enlightened supermarkets rarely carry more than twenty varieties in a year, and it has required legislation to ensure that even these are named.

The shelves are stocked with apples from across the world, while native trees have been grubbed up and burnt, and the orchards turned over to other uses. To walk round the Brogdale research station in Kent where the national library of trees is still kept (although it is under threat), is not just beautiful and inspiring, but also humiliating. That such a national heritage could be abandoned so easily, is a sobering reminder of how fragile is our own attachment to this earth.

To the cuisinier today, hues and shades of flavour still provide the dictionary, but it is a smaller and slimmer volume, despite the imports of exotics that falsely suggest otherwise.

COOKING ON THE FRONTIERS

To make a *beurre blanc* is to make a *beurre blanc*; to make a soufflé is to make a soufflé. Everyone can do it. The produce is now so standardized that two chefs 100 miles apart could still produce identical dishes, where Francoise Fayolle's five dishes were constantly differing. The kitchen does not have to wrestle with the daily, unnerving knowledge that the ingredients themselves are not trustworthy. Standardization has bred confidence. In turn, that confidence has pushed chefs to think in different ways. This may seem a small recipe from such a great modern chef as Raymond Blanc, but it captures, very simply, the values of contrast and approach that have become the tenets of the new brigades.

In a normal soufflé, the egg whites are loosely beaten so that it rises quickly. Here, the idea is to achieve the same texture, but without the mixture rising, so the egg whites are beaten stiffly and then cooked in a bain-marie. The soufflé is cooked twice, and the second baking produces a wonderful crust.

DUO DE SOUFFLÉ AU CABECOU ET
TERRINE DE ROQUEFORT

THE TERRINE: Drain 200g cottage cheese in a muslin cloth for 24 hours. Bring to the boiling point 50ml cream, dilute softened gelatine, cool. Mix 100ml sour cream and another 50ml cream with the cottage cheese. Taste, season with salt and freshly ground pepper.

Add 300g chopped, blanched walnuts, 30g diced celery, 30g diced apples. Mix thoroughly. Line the bottom and sides of terrine with cling film, leaving an overlap. Half-fill with the mixture.

Place 60g crumbled Roquefort in the middle of the terrine and cover with the remaining cottage cheese mix. Smooth the top with a spatula, and fold over the cling film. Refrigerate at least six hours.

THE SOUFFLÉ: Butter the inside of 8 ramekin dishes and cover the bottom and sides with breadcrumbs.

Make a béchamel sauce with 15g butter, 15g flour and 100ml milk. With the flat of a knife, cream 50g matured goat cheese (Cabecou if possible) and whisk it into the béchamel. Add 2 egg yolks.

Beat 4 egg whites to a light peak, add a generous pinch of salt, pepper and lemon juice, then beat mixture very tightly. Briskly whisk a quarter of the egg whites into the béchamel sauce, then very delicately fold in the remainder.

Spoon the mixture into the ramekins, one-third up, place 50g diced goat cheese in the middle of the soufflé mixture, then fill with the rest of the soufflé mixture.

Pre-heat oven to gas 3, 325°F (160°C), line a roasting tray with absorbent paper, and pour in water, 1cm deep. Bring to a boil, add soufflé and bake for 10 minutes. The soufflé will be barely cooked at this stage. Remove from the tray, and cool for 5 minutes. Place more breadcrumbs on the tray. Turn out the soufflé on to the breadcrumbs, and gently roll in them.

THE SALAD: Mix 1 tablespoon white wine vinegar, 3 tablespoons grapeseed oil, ½ tablespoon hazelnut oil, a pinch of salt, 4 turns freshly ground pepper and 1 finely chopped shallot into a vinaigrette. Lay 3 large handfuls of prepared salads over the liquid, but do not mix.

TO SERVE: Prepare 4 large plates. Unmould the terrine and remove cling film. Cut 8 slices with a knife that has been dipped in hot water. Place 2 slices on the left hand side of each plate. Place the unmoulded soufflés on a tray, and reheat in a very hot oven for 3–4 minutes. Mix the salads and vinaigrette, correct the seasoning, and place in the centre of the plates. Remove the soufflés from the oven and place on the right side of the salad.

Other cheeses can be used in place of goat. A well-matured Maroilles is effective, but should be used sparingly.

JASMIN AND LEMON

Much of modern cooking is about the relationships of flavour and taste, high and low, sweet and sour, hot and cold, smooth and silk, soft and hard. Not so long ago, when Bruno Loubet was cooking in a two-tier bistro at the bottom of the Fulham Road for a stunned and appreciative audience, who had some difficulty believing in what they were getting, a *crème brulée* was a *crème brulée*, the sort of thing found in hotel menus and trattorias with aspirations. Loubet took it on, and evolved a dish that is a subtle interaction of textures, smooth and granular, cold and hot, brittle and soft; and tastes: lemon, jasmin and almond. He is now head chef at the Inn on the Park in Mayfair, and has a Michelin rosette, but conceived this dessert while working for Blanc at Great Milton.

CRÈME BRULÉE AU CITRON, SORBET DE THÉ AU JASMIN AVEC TUILE D'AMANDE
AFTER BRUNO LOUBET

THE CRÈME: Extract the juice of 1 orange and 3 lemons. Add 50ml kirsch. Put 3 eggs and 1 yolk in a bowl with 150g soft brown sugar, and beat until the sugar melts. Add 150ml cream and the fruit juice. Fill the mixture into ramekins and cook in a bain-marie at gas 5, 375°F (190°C) for about 25 minutes. Leave to cool completely.

THE ALMOND TUILE: Cream 50g butter. Mix with 50g flour, 50g ground almonds, 350g sugar, and beat with the white of 6 eggs until smooth. Spread out thinly in teaspoons on greased baking sheet, and bake at gas 5, 375°F (190°C) for five minutes. Fold into cornets around a wooden spoon.

THE SORBET: Boil 250ml water with 50g sugar. Add 1 tablespoon jasmin tea, and leave to infuse until completely cold. Strain. Add 1 tablespoon egg white and turn in a sorbet machine.

TO SERVE: Cover the ramekin dishes with brown sugar. Heat the blade of a wide knife on the gas until very hot and burn the sugar with it. Serve with the sorbet on the side, in the almond tuile.

John Burton-Race worked in the original Summertown Quat' Saisons as number two, and took on the Petit Blanc when Raymond Blanc went to the Manoire, before finally moving into his own premises, L'Ortolan at Shinfield. This dish was conceived for the launch of the Egon Ronay guide book in 1988. He served first a small, restrained plate of three mousses, then followed it up with the larger, full text on meat-sized plates centred on huge fans of chocolate. It is a playful romp through the tomes of chocolate mousse and gâteau that have trundled along with cooking through the century. Carême and Escoffier might have approved of such fantasy.

THE PLATE OF THE MASTER CHOCOLATIER
AFTER JOHN BURTON-RACE (FOUR MINIATURIZED CHOCOLATE DESSERTS, WITH ORANGE AND PASSION FRUIT GRANITÉ)

1. MOGADOR: Mix 7g almonds with 75g icing sugar and whisk in 65g eggs and 40g egg yolks. Whisk 140g egg white with 50g sugar. Fold 50g flour and 10g cocoa powder into the almond mix and add the whisked whites. Spread on to silicone paper and bake at gas 4, 350°F (180°C) for approximately 12 minutes.

THE SYRUP: Combine 100g stock syrup, 40g raspberry *eau de vie* and 40g water.

THE MOGADOR MOUSSE Melt 100g couverture chocolate and 15g cocoa paste. Separately, bring 15g cocoa paste, 35g water and cocoa powder to the boil. Whisk on to 75g egg yolks and cook as for a sabayon, then add 5g softened gelatine and whisk in machine until soft. Add a little whipped cream to the chocolate mix, whisk and fold in 125g Italian meringue, the cooled sabayon and finally some more whipped cream.

TO SERVE: Place a disc of chocolate biscuit sponge in base of circle, and lightly soak with the raspberry syrup. Brush with a thin layer of raspberry jam. Pipe in a layer of mousse, and stud the centre with several raspberries soaked in raspberry liquor. Garnish the circle to rim, and smooth over the surface. Freeze. Glaze the surface with hot, seeded, raspberry jam. Remove from circle. Serve with raspberry coulis once defrosted.

2. FINESSE DE PARIS: Mix together 125g icing sugar, 125g ground almonds, 35g flour. Add 10g sugar to 170g eggs and progressively whisk into dry ingredients. Continue until light and fluffy, then fold in 25g cooled, melted butter. Whisk 110g egg whites with 20g sugar and, when firm, fold into the almond mixture. Spread out on to silicone paper and bake at gas 2, 275°F (140°C) for approximately 6 minutes.

VANILLA SYRUP: Combine 125g of water, 85g sugar, ½ split vanilla pod, and bring to the boil.

MILK CHOCOLATE MOUSSE: Melt 100g milk chocolate. Bring boiling stock syrup to a bowl, and whisk into 30g egg yolks. Cook as for a sabayon, then whisk on machine until cool. Add a little whipped cream to the chocolate. Whisk, then fold in the sabayon and finally some more whipping cream.

LIGHT VANILLA MOUSSE: Make a sabayon with 85g yolks and 75g syrup. Flavour with vanilla extract. Add 2g melted gelatine and fold in 125g whipped cream. Keep back a little sabayon.

TO SERVE: Place a disc of joconde biscuit sponge in the base of a circle, and lightly soak with vanilla syrup. Garnish the circle to half its depth with milk chocolate mousse. Allow to set. Fill the rim with vanilla mousse, and smooth over the surface. Refrigerate, then remove circle. Cover the sides with a fine layer of milk chocolate. For the surface, cut a disc of joconde biscuit of the same size. Spread over a thin layer of sabayon. Dust with sugar, and glaze with caramelizing iron. Serve with chocolate sauce.

3. CRÉOLE
CHOCOLATE MERINGUE: Whisk 75g egg whites with 75g sugar to a firm meringue, then fold in 70g sifted icing sugar and 10g cocoa powder. Using a small plain nozzle, pipe out discs of a slightly smaller diameter, to the size of the circle to be used. Bake for approximately 45 minutes in a low oven.

CHOCOLATE MOUSSE: Melt together 50g bittersweet and 50g semi-couverture chocolate, whisk in 50g unsalted butter and then 20g egg yolks. Whisk 60g egg whites with 25g sugar until firm, and fold delicately into the cool chocolate mixture.

TO SERVE: Place a meringue disc in the base of the circle. Garnish with chocolate mousse. Place a second meringue disc on to mousse. Cover to rim of circle, and smooth over the surface. Refrigerate, remove circle and decorate the sides and surface with a fine layer of chocolate leaves, using dark couverture. Serve with a vanilla anglaise.

4. MIROIR AUX GRIOTTINES
SYRUP: Combine 100g stock syrup, 40g kirsch and 40g water.

WHITE CHOCOLATE MOUSSE: Melt 100g white chocolate and a little whipped cream and whisk until smooth, then fold in more cream so that in total it is 2 parts cream to 1 part chocolate.

TO SERVE: Place a disc of chocolate biscuit sponge in the base of the circle and lightly soak with kirsch syrup. Pipe in a layer of mousse and stud the centre with griottine cherries. Garnish to the circle rim and smooth over the surface. Refrigerate, remove circle and decorate the surface with a disc of fine tempered white chocolate. Serve with a cherry coulis.

5. PASSION FRUIT AND ORANGE GRANITÉ
Combine the clarified juice of 2 oranges, the juice of 8 passion fruit and 50g of stock syrup. Pour into a flat tray and freeze.

6. THE SERVICE
Finish the presentation of this dessert with a centrepiece of a chocolate shell made using dark-tempered couverture. A suitably sized mould can be wrapped in cling film and dipped in the couverture. When it has hardened, carefully remove from the mould and peel away the cling film. At the time of service, place each individual miniature dessert on the plate, with its accompanying sauce. Position the chocolate shell in the centre and garnish with a passion fruit and orange granité, covered with a sugar cage.

POSTSCRIPT

MODERN COOKING IS not *better* than classical or regional cooking. It is different, because the challenges it faces are different. The move towards healthier eating is inevitable, because we do not do so much physical work today, and the houses we live in are properly heated. Good food, we expect, should be food that is good for us.

The standardizing of supply lines has improved quality, in one sense. As in Burton-Race's chocolate extravaganza, with cocoa from Central America, passion fruit from Kenya, techniques from France, machines from Germany, hands from England, the idea of the global market appears, superficially, to triumph.

But in reality, as we have seen with apples, other fruits and vegetables, and animal breeds, this standardization has also cut back the choice available, to the point where abundance has come to mean bleak uniformity. Quality today means a single thing, where a hundred years ago it meant a thousand things. That in itself is an issue for all of us, not just the professional kitchen.

One conclusion has been very hard to escape, in writing this book. To make such so-called progress possible, it has been necessary to supplement foods with artificial colours, preservatives and flavours in order to make them acceptable. We are becoming junkies hooked on these additives, and are no longer able or willing to discriminate between them and subtler natural tastes. You have only to look at a child, to see that a packet of sweets, concentrated with sugar, the colour improved, the wrapping carefully conceived, is a more persuasive product than a pear or an apple.

Such foods and policies arise directly out of the collapse of the British food industry, by which I mean the craft industries allied to the restaurant.

It is often asked, why is British food so poor? And despite the very real revival described in these pages, it is a charge that still sticks. It sticks, because there has been no political will to stop the decline which began with a generation being taken off the land to fight the first world war. It sticks, because the influence of rationing is still imprinted on older people's minds. It sticks, because the people responsible for polluting the food chain – initially the coastline and rivers and, more recently, the fields – have not been stopped. For most of us, these things happen just out of sight, but in the kitchen they are plain to see.

A more encouraging conclusion, however, has also presented itself.

Most of the people mentioned in this book, and the many I have had to leave out, have not graduated from a single school. They come from many different backgrounds, and have reached similar points from different perspectives. What they share is a common value, which was Point's value and also, to some extent, an old English one: that the produce should speak for itself.

To the intelligent kitchen, it can hardly be enough any more to just repeat and repeat a few dishes. That was catering. Once that simplistic notion is thrown away, then each day, or certainly each season, comes back into its own. That is cooking.

END PIECE

Recipe from Raymond Thuilier, friend of Fernand Point, and chef patron of Oustau de Baumanière now run by his grandson, for a beetroot sauce to go with grilled fish.

1. Wash it.

2. Cook it.

3. Peel it.

4. Liquidize it.

RECIPES INDEX

RESTAURANTS INDEX